Regan Arts.

65 Bleecker Street
New York, NY 10012

Copyright © 2016 by The Rookie Handbook Team, LLC

First Regan Arts edition, September 2016

Library of Congress Control Number: 2016939702

ISBN 978-1-68245-034-5

Interior and cover design and illustrations by Matt Stevens

Printed in China

10 9 8 7 6 5 4 3 2 1

CONTENTS

FOREWORD

As you get set to take your journey into this important work—and "journey" is an accurate assessment of your impending experience (so is the word "experience")—please do know this: Ryan Kalil and Jordan Gross do *not* hate rookies. Well, Geoff Hangartner might. I don't know Geoff all that well, but if Kalil and Gross back his play as an F.O.R. (Friend of Rookies), well, then I'm on board. Plus, in Carolina, these three guys protected Cam Newton in what turned out to be one of the greatest rookie seasons in NFL quarterbacking history. Now look at Cam. He's an MVP dabbing all over the place. And on dem folks.

So, if this distinguished trio of offensive linemen were so offended by rookies, why would they then write a smarm-filled primer called The Rookie Handbook?

Let's be real. Just because the pages that follow make it seem as if rookies are a target of their derision, disgust, and disrespect (the dreaded Three Ds), it's truly not the case. This book is an actual guide—a road map, if you will—on how one can smartly identify and avoid rookie problems, which, historically and generally, has been a pretty large problem for rookies. And not just in the NFL. Neophytes everywhere would be well-advised to read this tome and take note of what lies in between the lines of the surprisingly cogent and superbly sarcastic prose penned by Kalil and Gross. Oh, yes, and by Hangartner, who Kalil and Gross tell me knows how to write. And read. Although, he's probably the reason there are so many illustrations in the book.

At any rate, take my word for it. We've all been rookies at one point or another, in whatever our endeavors. So *The Rookie Handbook* will help you. This handbook will help NFL rookies. And, ultimately, by helping you and those crucial newcomers to the NFL, your authors Ryan Kalil, Jordan Gross, and Geoff Hangartner are helping America. Or fantasy football drafters silly enough to risk a high pick on some clueless rookie.

Feel good that you've picked up this book. And enjoy. I personally guarantee its freshness.

—RICH EISEN

TO THE ROOKIES IN ALL WALKS OF LIFE &
EVERYONE GIVING IT THEIR BEST SHOT

Welcome to *The Rookie Handbook*, the most comprehensive look inside the life of an NFL rookie ever produced. Its purpose is to help you avoid the common pitfalls most first-time professionals find themselves in. Reading this book will not guarantee that you get drafted, become a starter, or even make the team. This book consists of the bare essentials of what should be a guide to better prepare you and make you feel comfortable in this new environment. And, while we've provided a great deal of valuable information, much was left out for you to discover for yourself.

In constructing *The Rookie Handbook* we realized early on that many of you were not the most scholarly of students and reading may not be your forte. So we took it upon ourselves to present the simplest version we could possibly conceive. The result is an easy-to-read, heavily illustrated reference book that should help you not only increase your chances of surviving your first season, but also of achieving a long and successful NFL career.

Enjoy . . . rookie.

Sincerely,

The Rookie Handbook Team

THE ROOKIE

AT A GLANCE

A. Although you may think you know everything, you don't. Pay attention, listen, and get in your damn playbook.

B. There's a chance you or some of your fellow rookies will be bankrupt or nearly there about two years after your careers end. Be smart with your money and don't become another statistic.

C. You're in the NFL. Congrats! But now everybody wants a piece of you. You need to learn to give your time to those who really care about you and avoid those interested in your fame or fortune.

D. Nerves are normal. If you're not nervous, something's wrong. If you're too nervous, something's wrong. Relax, it's not quantum physics . . . it's still just football.

E. Few sports demand the same strength, speed, and agility needed to succeed in the pros. Take your body seriously, put away the cheese puffs, get off the video games, and start training for professional football. After all, it's only the greatest opportunity you'll probably ever have.

SECTION 01
PRE-DRAFT

WHERE TO DO YOUR PRE-DRAFT
TRAINING

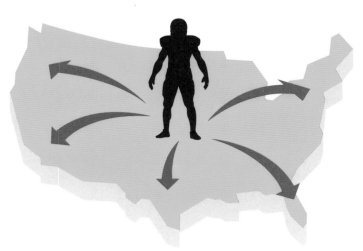

Once your final college game is over, your preparation for the draft begins immediately. One of your biggest decisions in preparing for the combine and pro day will be where you should train.

If you've already selected an agent, they'll likely suggest some fancy training facility that specializes in preparing athletes for the NFL draft process. These programs can be beneficial, providing great perks such as massage therapists or customized nutrition plans, but they typically do little to no *football* training. Their goal is to prepare you for the running and jumping tests at the combine and pro day. Work with your agent to find someone to teach you the football techniques necessary for success at the pro level.

Your other option is to stay and work with the meathead strength coaches at your (former) university. They will know you and your strengths and weaknesses best, but will likely not give you their full attention since their top priority is getting next year's freshmen ready for college football. There are no clear-cut answers as to where you should train, but your goal should be to minimize the distractions and find a place with coaches who will push you to be your best, not tell you how great you are.

SELECTING A
SPORTS AGENT

Let's be very frank about sports agents: They *cannot* get you drafted. A good agent is someone who can prepare you for the upcoming "meat grinder" of evaluations and, most importantly, negotiate a solid contract for you, or rather . . . "SHOW YOU THE MONEY!" Here are a few kinds of agents who are going to be courting you once you declare for the draft. Choose wisely.

FAMILY AGENT
Great, your uncle Joe watched every one of your games in college. Why does this give him the right to a percentage of your total contract?

WANNABE COOL AGENT
He's cool, and he'll let you know it with his clothes and his lingo. Make sure his negotiating skills are as fresh as his wardrobe.

ESTABLISHED AGENT
He's an industry legend, has struck some huge deals, and may or may not have time for you.

DOUBLE-DOWN-ON-YOU AGENT
He needs you more than he'll ever let on and he's eager to please. Often seen juggling twenty things at once.

FLASHY BLING AGENT
Known for going out of his way to impress you with all of the finer things. Better hope you get drafted, because, one way or another, you're paying him back for everything you thought was on his tab.

FORMER PLAYER AGENT
Known for his shiny Super Bowl ring, which he keeps flashing in your face, and his years of NFL experience. OK, but does he know how to negotiate off-season workout bonuses?

CHOOSING YOUR
WORKOUT ATTIRE

The 40-yard dash is easily the most famous and most watched measurable of them all. The current trend is for players to minimize drag and friction by wearing just spandex. News flash . . . it doesn't help. Keep in mind, coaches love an impressive physique, so if your intent of running half-naked is to show off the bod, good thinking. However, for those of you with chubbier, less-defined-looking bodies: Keep the clothes on. A hundredth of a second is not worth a lifetime of embarrassing photos of your jiggly body parts crossing the finish line.

40-YD. DASH

4.82
SECONDS

IN YOUR MIND

40-YD. DASH

5.82
SECONDS

IN REALITY

POKE AND PROD
DOCTOR EXAMS

The combine is filled with hours of MRIs, X-rays, and drug tests. Once you survive that gauntlet, you might think that the worst is behind you, but they save the best for last—the dreaded poke-and-prod doctor exams.

"What is that?" you ask. Thirty-two different team medical staff members will each be given a hands-on opportunity to check out the stability and health of your entire body. Did you have a shoulder injury your sophomore year? Expect every doctor to tug and pull on your arm like Rowdy Roddy Piper. A grade 1 MCL sprain last season? Don't worry; it'll be a grade 3 by the time they get done with you.

You need to understand that these teams are considering investing a lot of money in you. Their team's medical staff is paid to assess your overall wellness and to report back with the most accurate picture possible, not to make you comfortable or happy.

ADVICE: Unless you have a serious injury, don't show that anything physically bothers you. Answer their questions honestly, but don't go full-disclosure with a complete medical history of everything you've ever hurt. Their job is to assess you; your job is to sell yourself. After you are done, take some Advil and ice up, son!

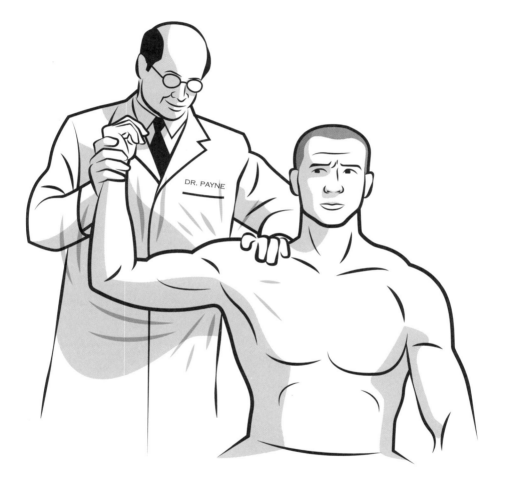

INTERVIEWS
WITH COACHES

At the combine you'll get your chance to run, lift, jump, and display your skills like a show pony. More importantly, you'll get a chance to meet with the teams that may be interested in drafting you.

These meetings are typically fifteen-minutes long. Sometimes, you may enter a team interview room and meet with just a few coaches. Other times, you might walk into a room filled with any combination of the following decision makers: the owner, GM, head coach, offensive and defensive coordinators, position coach, trainer, player development coordinator, head of security, and legendary former players. Be on time and look presentable. This is a job interview. Understand that the impression you leave with this team can elevate or lower your draft status.

Teams want to know everything about you. Interviews can range from an informal chat to an intense Xs and Os session. At times they get pretty personal, making erroneous claims or interrogating you like you were involved in a bank heist. It all depends on the organization and your individual history.

ADVICE: Be yourself. Teams hate scripted answers. Highlight your love of the game, especially if asked about your ambitions post-football. Mention that you want to get into coaching. Coaches love players who eat, sleep, and breathe football. They don't want to hear about your passion for commercial real estate or your dreams of starting a new record label.

SECTION 02
THE DRAFT

TAKING STOCK OF
DRAFT STOCK

Why does one publication predict you'll be a second-round draft pick and another suggest you should have stayed one more year in school? Which analyst should you listen to since one is saying your lack of speed will scare teams away while the other is declaring teams are gushing over your incredible explosiveness?

The truth is, no one really knows how the draft will unfold. Draft day trades and players slipping down the draft board can cause teams to change plans at a moment's notice. It's almost impossible to find a subjective, unbiased person or service that can provide you a realistic expectation for what will happen on draft day. Your agent may be optimistic about when you will be selected, but plenty of draft day promises have been broken.

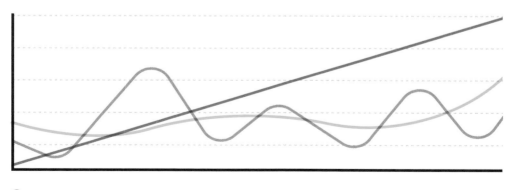

- YOUR AGENT
- TOP FOOTBALL PUBLICATION
- TALKING HEAD ANALYST

WHERE TO SPEND
YOUR BIG DAY

THE GREEN ROOM
If you're lucky enough to get invited to the draft, there's a good chance you will be a high pick. Just remember, there is a chance of you dropping on the draft board and being the guy "stuck in the green room."

THE GETAWAY
Easily the least stressful environment. Still, try to be available in case a potential team wants to have one last chat with you before they make their pick.

The big day is finally here. You think you know what's going to happen and everyone and their mom has told you who's drafting you. The truth is, nobody knows and a lot of guys won't get the phone call. Draft day is friggin' stressful! Who you decide to spend the day with and where can either add or subtract to that stress. Here are a few of the most common ways players choose to spend their big day.

HOMETOWN PARTY

This can be a great celebration with everyone you've ever known, from high school friends to your local pastor and his family. It can also quickly become the most stressful, awkward, and embarrassing event of your life if you don't get drafted.

SMALL GET-TOGETHER

Probably the best way to spend a day of uncertainty. Being at home with only those in your immediate circle can really help calm the nerves while you await your football fate.

DRAFTED

You were probably a great college football player, the best player on your team, maybe even the country. For months leading up to the draft, your family, friends, fans, and agent have been telling you how great you are. Finally, you get the call from the team that just drafted you: "Hey, stud, you want to help us go win a Super Bowl?"

Feeling pretty good about yourself, huh? You should, but once this day is through, make sure to remember that the real work has yet to begin. No one cares about your college career anymore. This is a show-me league and you will now be playing against individuals who at one time were also the best college football players in the country. Confidence is great, but don't be so arrogant to think that the transition to pro football will be a walk in the park.

ADVICE: Don't get worked up over what pick you were in the draft. You can't change it now, so move on. Unless you were the first pick, everyone feels slighted by the teams that passed them up.

UNDRAFTED

Unfortunately, Mr. Irrelevant has been selected and the draft is over without your name being called. You will now have to enter the professional ranks as an undrafted rookie. While not being drafted might make your road to stardom a little tougher, it does not mean you can't have a great career. One positive to being undrafted is the ability to choose where you sign. Evaluate the teams interested in you and, instead of picking a team based on weather and location, take into account current depth charts, schemes, and coaching style in an effort to find the one where you have the best shot at making the roster.

ADVICE: Don't get worked up over not being drafted. Plenty of former and current All-Pros weren't drafted. It's not where you start; it's what you do with the opportunities you are given, however limited they may be.

SECTION 03
FINANCES

CONTRACT

All you want to know is when you can sign the dotted line and get your first big check. Slow down, rookie—contracts can be a huge distraction if all you think about is your big payday. Fortunately for you, rookie contracts have become very standardized, so the chances of a holdout are almost nonexistent. Still, beyond salary negations, there is the occasional matter of curious contract language. From prohibiting interstellar travel to apocalyptic "End of the World" clauses, some teams and players have requested strange provisions to sweeten the deal. As long as you have consulted the section about choosing the right agent, you will be fine. Let the agent worry about the negotiations and you work on making the team.

FINANCIAL ADVISORS & LOANS

SELECTING A FINANCIAL ADVISOR

Just because you have money doesn't make you a businessman. Now that your agent has negotiated your rookie deal, you will soon have some real coin in your pockets. Not sure what to do with it? Don't worry; there will be lots of long-lost family members and greasy financial advisors knocking down your door with "amazing" investment ideas on how to turn your thousands into millions, or millions into billions. Beware of anything that sounds too good to be true and stay away from timeshares in the Bahamas! This is likely your first experience with investing, so seek advice from someone you trust who has real experience. Never do anything that makes you uncomfortable; it's your money, after all.

PRE-DRAFT LOANS

One of the biggest mistakes that penniless NFL prospects make prior to the draft? Taking out loans with the misguided certainty that they will get signed, make a lot of money, and be able to quickly pay off any pre-draft debt. Sadly, the truth is that many rookies who borrow money are not drafted and soon find themselves in a huge financial hole.

The money you're asking for or being offered by an agent is not a gift. You'll have to pay it back at some point. So resist the temptation and live like a poor college student for a few more months. Driving around in a brand new SUV for three months is not worth the risk of failing to make a roster, leaving you with loads of debt.

THE PRO DISCOUNT

FOR PROS ONLY... 200%
TWICE AS MUCH!
THE PRO DISCOUNT

Sometimes, it's a good idea to give as little information as possible about what you do for a living. When people find out that you are a professional athlete, many will assume you're rolling in the dough. Maybe you are, maybe you're not. Many times, when someone finds out you can afford to pay their asking price, they'll want you to pay it, and then some.

If it's important to you to preserve your hard-earned dough, then do your due diligence just like everyone else. There are lots of honest, hardworking folks who would gladly give you something practically for free just to do business with you. If you don't want to spend the time to get multiple quotes, research, or ask around . . . then you deserve to be ripped off.

REAL MONEY

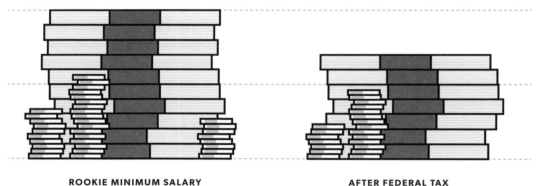

ROOKIE MINIMUM SALARY

AFTER FEDERAL TAX
(-39.6%)

After years of playing for free, you are finally getting paid to play football. Congratulations! It's easy to be excited about the money that you are now making, but don't be an idiot. All of your friends and family may have their hands out, but so do Uncle Sam and your agent. General rule: consider one half of your money gone due to taxes and fees. While you are making great money and certainly outearning your former college classmates, you aren't set financially for the rest of your life just yet.

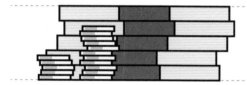

AFTER STATE TAX
(- 0 – 13.3% Depending on Residence)

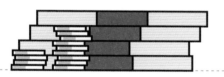

AFTER AGENT FEES
(2 – 3%)

DREAM CAR

Many players aren't tempted to buy designer bags, custom jewelry, or even big fancy houses. But almost every rookie, regardless of their future earnings, has the impulse to purchase the car of their dreams. If you can afford to buy yourself a nice new set of wheels, try to at least contain yourself. Most rookies aren't content until they've customized every inch of their new ride. Honestly, there's a strong chance that you will lose interest in your "dream car" when it eventually becomes outdated. When the time comes to sell your personal statement on wheels, hopefully there's a buyer out there who really wants a neon-yellow truck with your name embroidered on the headrests and a mural of you lying next to a tiger painted on the hood.

THE *"PULL ME OVER"* PACKAGE:

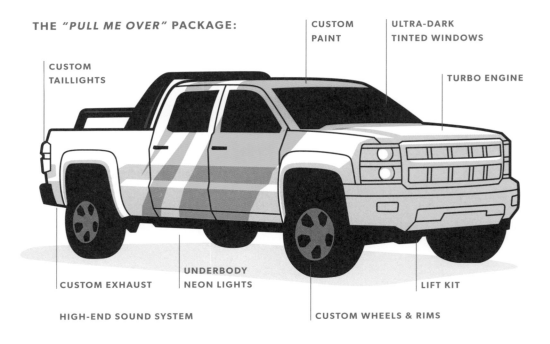

CUSTOM PAINT

ULTRA-DARK TINTED WINDOWS

CUSTOM TAILLIGHTS

TURBO ENGINE

CUSTOM EXHAUST

UNDERBODY NEON LIGHTS

LIFT KIT

HIGH-END SOUND SYSTEM

CUSTOM WHEELS & RIMS

FUGAZI

Public perception is that every player has deep pockets and will purchase the grandest things money can buy. Unfortunately, this is true about many players, but others will actually use this cliché to their advantage. The smart individuals are content with owning valuables that . . . aren't really all that valuable. Why spend thousands of dollars on diamond stud earrings when you can buy cubic zirconia ones for a few bucks? They are basically identical in appearance and, because you are a ball player, everyone will assume they're the real deal anyway. Protect your finances and resist the urge to waste your money on, say, an overpriced, designer cotton-blend tee that costs more than two months of rent.

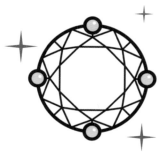

REAL DIAMOND
CARAT WEIGHT - 3.11
COLOR GRADE - H
CLARITY GRADE - SI1

$100,700

FAKE DIAMOND
LARGE STUD DIAMETER - 7 MM
SETTING - PRONG
COLOR - WHITE

$22

THE DEMAND FOR
TICKETS

Tickets are a big distraction for players and coaches during the season. People you haven't seen in years will come out of the woodwork looking for tickets to your games, especially if you play a game near your hometown. Tickets are *not* free. You will get *two* free tickets for home games and none for games on the road. You pay full price (no player discount), and there will be a deadline to request tickets usually, three or four days before the game. Set the expectations for tickets early in your career. It's okay to tell people that you can't or won't get them tickets. You can't please everyone; don't try. Make an effort to handle all ticket requests early in the week so you aren't dealing with them on game day.

3:48
Monday, November 22

Aunt Janet
Looking for tickets!

Ben Smith
Hey buddy. Need two for Sunday!

Mark Ward
Any extras this week?

Uncle Harvey
NEED...TICKETS! TICKETS! TICKETS!

Robert Jones
Guess who?! Any extra tickets this week?

Grandma
In town and hoping to go to game

EXPECTATIONS ABOUT
ENDORSEMENTS

Shoe deals, free cell phone service, or maybe even a car to drive during the season? Sounds amazing, huh? Endorsement deals are a great way to make a little extra cash or get cool stuff for free, but be aware of the strings attached. The people giving you this stuff will want something in return, usually involving your limited free time. Make sure you know what they expect from you before you sign on the dotted line.

ROOKIE DUTIES

AND RITES OF PASSAGE

TRADITIONS

Not all locker-room traditions are the same. Some have been around for decades, while others died with the departure of long-tenured former players or coaching staff. There are, however, a few traditions that have been constant through the years. If the tradition exists where you are playing, get it done. Don't be the rookie who draws the ire of veterans by not doing what is asked of you. Here are a few commonplace traditions you should be aware of.

CARRYING PADS AND HELMETS

You've just finished practice and you're exhausted. Guess what? Your rookie duties don't end with practice. You're young and full of stamina and now the older players in your position group are going to take advantage of that by making you carry their pads into the locker room. Believe us, it's a pain in the ass, especially if there are a lot of guys in your position group. Stack those shoulder pads on your own, claw as many helmets by the facemask as you can, and suck it up. It's only for a season and it's all part of the rite of passage. Oh, by the way, don't forget your own pads.

DOUGHNUTS AND COFFEE

Many teams in the league have the tradition of rookies bringing in doughnuts and coffee for the team to enjoy prior to practice the day before the game. Although players work to perfect their bodies and to be in peak shape for the most physically demanding and challenging sport . . . who can say no to a delicious sweetened and glazed ring of deep-fried dough?

PRACTICE EQUIPMENT

Your duties as a rookie are not limited to the locker room. They extend to the practice field as well. Moving sleds, tackling dummies, pads, boards, nets, and any other apparatus your position group might require is your responsibility. Don't whine, complain, or move slowly. Get your rookie butt in gear and go grab what is needed, because the older guys sure as hell aren't doing it!

TOWELS FOR THE VETS

As a veteran player, there's nothing better after practice than finding a freshly folded towel on your chair like you're at a five-star resort. The symbolism of veteran status is equally as gratifying as the convenience of not having to find a towel for yourself. Make sure you are consistent. Vets love a routine and have little patience for those who disrupt it. It's tedious now, but, after your rookie season, it's nice to be on the receiving end of this tradition.

ROOKIE DINNER

For decades, rookies have had the "honor" of taking their position group out for a nice meal during their rookie season. Kobe steaks, lobster, champagne, caviar. You get the picture. The cost of your rookie dinner will depend solely on the oldest players in your position group. Are you a practice-squad rookie who takes home a fraction of what a drafted player makes? If the veterans are fair and just, they may consider this and adjust the food and beverage orders accordingly. But if they are completely unreasonable people? Then you might be playing for free that month.

ROOKIE HAIRCUTS

Which would you choose if you were given the option of singing in front of your team, performing a comedy skit, or letting the veterans select a new hairstyle for you? Surprisingly, many rookies choose the new hairstyle.

The rookie haircut is a veterans' favorite, mostly because of how funny and harmless it is in nature. There's a slim chance you'll experience any sort of lifelong psychological trauma because of a heinous haircut. It's temporary. Your hair will grow back.

To get a sense of what you may be in for, here's a look at the most popular hairstyles that trim their way atop the scalps of rookies every year.

ISLANDS IN THE STREAM

DIG-DUG

THE FRIAR TUCK

THE HERO WE DESERVE

HEY MOE

THE ROAD NOT TAKEN

PARTY IN THE BACK

BLACK FRIDAY

SHOCK & AWE

INITIATION BY SONG

♫

Everyone knows that NFL teams use the long slog that is training camp to "initiate" their rookies. For most teams, keeping things light by having rookies sing for them is a tradition as old as the game itself.

Here's what typically happens. One day at lunch or prior to a meeting, a veteran player will call you out to stand up on your chair and sing a song. Announce the song and artist you will be singing. Motown's always a hit. Stay away from anything too far from mainstream; guys love to sing along. Make sure you know the lyrics. There is nothing more pathetic than a grown man who can't remember the words to a song and has to resort to singing "Happy Birthday" or "I'm a Little Teapot."

Once you begin, be loud and proud. If you can hold a tune, great. If you can't, great. Either way, you will be well-received if you belt out the notes like you're James Brown live at the Apollo. Have fun with it and put on a performance.

Vets are constantly trying to figure out how you are going to respond when the pressure is on. Leading a group of men singing "Ain't Too Proud to Beg" while they enjoy a delicious Salisbury steak and a Gatorade will take you one step closer to proving you belong.

THE RIGHT WAY

PRESEASON

PRESEASON
GAME TAPE

Every coach in the league will say some version of this: "You aren't just trying to make this team! There are thirty-one other teams that'll be watching these games!" Throughout the preseason, your current team has been evaluating you in practices, walk-throughs, meetings, and the exhibition games. Other potential employers will only have access to your game tapes. Strong play in preseason games is essential to give yourself the best chance at making your current team or creating your next opportunity if you are released.

TRAINING CAMP
ESSENTIALS

According to the NFL, more than half of the NFL teams stay at home for training camp. For those on teams that hold training camp elsewhere, here is a list of camp essentials vetted by veterans with years of training camp experience:

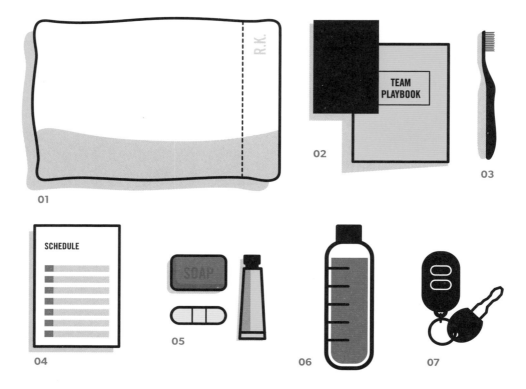

01 PERSONAL PILLOW

Sleep is your greatest ally. Bringing your own pillow from home will increase your chances of a good night's sleep.

02 ENTERTAINMENT

With the limited downtime you're provided, it's best to use that time to rest. TVs, cell phones, and computers can help pass the time, but science shows prolonged light exposure before sleep can disrupt body rhythms and suppress the release of the hormone melatonin, which promotes quality slumber time. We recommend bringing a book or maybe just spending some time in your playbook before bed.

03 TOOTHBRUSH

Bacteria attacking your enamel couldn't care less about how many passes you caught or tackles you've made. Just because we are coached to be tough, aggressive, and intimidating doesn't mean we should ignore regular oral hygiene. Seriously, brush your teeth.

04 SCHEDULE

Know the schedule and be early. Nothing creates a worse impression than being late to meetings, treatment, or practice. Another reason to be early is to beat the older players. In the NFL, there is an unwritten "seniority" rule that players older than you get preferential treatment. So be early; don't use the excuse "I didn't know." If you're not sure, ask a veteran player.

05 CUTS, WOUNDS & BLISTERS

Because we play a contact sport, football players are prone to staph infections. The frequency of cuts and the warm, moist conditions in locker rooms encourage the growth of this super-antibiotic-resistant bacteria that can cause serious infections. Good hygiene is the most effective way to prevent staph infections, so stay on top of openings in the skin and keep them clean and covered until they're healed.

06 HYDRATION

It's vitally important to stay properly hydrated before, during, and after practices. Let's quickly recap the importance of water: It regulates your body temperature, lubricates joints, and helps transport nutrients for energy and recovery. Seems like common sense, but many athletes take it for granted. A common rule of thumb to stay hydrated is to drink 16 oz. of water or sports drink for every pound you lose after practice. In addition to water, you need to replenish your electrolytes. Gatorlytes aren't the greatest tasting things, but they are a quick and easy way to get your body some extra sodium and potassium.

07 CARPOOL

Nothing builds camaraderie with a new teammate like sharing a drive to camp. Also, limiting distractions is important during your time of fighting for a job, so something as small as not worrying about your automobile can go a long way.

TRAVEL ATTIRE

Many teams require their players to wear a suit and tie for away-game travel and/or team functions. It would be wise to own a suit if you don't already. If you want to make a fashion statement with hats, handkerchiefs, fur, gator, and a man purse as a rookie . . . fine, but wear at your own risk.

CAMP CLOTHES

Most first-year players make the mistake of packing for camp like a two-month vacation. You're with the same guys every day and most of them will probably wear the same outfit multiple days in a row. If you are a keen observer, you'll notice that the older players bring the least amount of stuff. Don't be afraid to pack light and wear the same shirt more than once. But, please bring enough underwear for each day of camp . . . you're a football player, not an animal.

TRANSPORTATION

Depending on the team you're on and where training camp is held, you may be in for weeks of long walks from dorms to meetings to the locker room to practice to the training table and back to the dorms. Walking is not a hard task, but just wait till you're two weeks into training camp. Common forms of transportation at remote training camp facilities include bicycles, Segways, and golf carts. As a first-year player, find out from an established player what is organizationally acceptable before you decide to rent some obnoxious ATV.

OVERPACKED!

GO TEAM!

SECRET HALFTIME FOOD

If you are good enough to be a starter during the preseason as a rookie, continue reading. If not, skip ahead, because this section doesn't apply to you. As you know by now, the rep count for playing in the preseason is decided ahead of time. Veteran players usually know approximately how long they will be playing before the game even starts. In any game in which they will not be playing after halftime, the players arrange for food to be ready for them to eat during intermission.

This food is typically hot dogs, burgers, or sandwiches and is secretly hidden in the equipment room. Access to this exclusive club is by invitation only. Don't expect the menu to be posted on the walls of the locker room or the head coach to announce what is available. If you're invited by a vet to partake in the bounty, then enjoy every minute of it. Keep all your actions stealthy and don't be a distraction. The rest of the team is most likely just around the corner preparing for the second half of the action. Keep this on the down low and make sure you don't have any ketchup on your face before you head back out onto the field.

PRACTICE

PRACTICE TEMPO

Every practice will have a specified tempo. The tempo means the speed at which the coach wants you to go. Within a specific practice, the tempo may change to get the results the coach wants. Know the speed of practice. Nothing pisses off coaches or players more than a guy who can't figure out the tempo. However, if you're not sure, err on the side of going too hard. You want to be told to gear it down, not to pick it up. Here are definitions of different tempos.

WALK-THROUGH (FULL PADS, HALF PADS, HATS):
Focus on stance and alignments, footwork, and technique. Walking/jogging pace through your assignments. No contact at all.

THUD (HALF PADS):
Full speed until you're about to make contact, then cut down your speed. Finish the play with a focus on avoiding contact and injury. No tackling, no pancake blocks. Stay off the QB.

THUD (FULL PADS):
Full speed up through contact with the understanding that no one should be purposely put to the ground. No tackling, no pancake blocks. Don't touch the QB.

LIVE (FULL PADS):
Game-type speed and contact. Full blocking and tackling up until the whistle. However, still not allowed to touch the QB! (See section on quickest way to get cut.)

FIGHT STRATEGY

Football is a game of aggression, and sometimes tempers rise high. Whether it's the end of training camp, late in the season, or some new guy off the street trying to make a name for himself, fights are bound to happen at practice. Chances are you will find yourself caught up in one. Players and coaches are impressed by good football players, not good fighters. However, a bad fighting performance in a mid-practice skirmish can lower your street cred. Stick to these simple fundamentals to preserve your safety and reputation.

STEP 1

Make sure your helmet is on and your chin strap is buckled. Never take it off.

STEP 2

Go for their face mask! If you can vice-grip your opponent's face mask, you can control both spacing and their movement.

STEP 3

A typical practice fight lasts only about 30 seconds. Your job is to hold up until the fight is broken up. We don't recommend throwing punches, but, if you must, try to use the open-hand head slap. A closed fist to the helmet is a good way to break your hand and end your season.

Side note: Other proven methods are knees to the body and takedowns (either by face-mask pulls to the ground or by grabbing a leg, pulling to the sky, and pushing your opponent to the ground).

Hand is nice and open to avoid hurting those fingers. Big-league technique on display.

BEWARE OF THESE PRACTICE
PLAYER TYPES

THE SCOUT-TEAM ALL-AMERICAN

As a rookie, you will undoubtedly be asked to be on the scout team at one time or another. Scout-team players are supposed to prepare their teammates for what is expected from that week's opponent, either during a walk-through or live practice.

The "Scout Team All-American," also known as "Rudy," is the guy who thinks the scout-team period is about them. Instead of giving a good look and doing what's on the card, Rudy goes rogue and tries to stand out by making up his own assignments and techniques to make a play.

This isn't a movie. Doing your own thing not only wrecks the period, but it can also get somebody hurt. Being a scout-team player doesn't mean you have to give half-ass effort or let the other player beat you, but you're there to service the starters. You can prepare your teammates for the game and still give great effort.

THE NO-PADS ALL-AMERICAN

The "No-Pads All-American" is not too dissimilar from the "Scout-Team All-American." You've never seen this player make plays in full-padded practices or games, but this player shines when the tempo slows way down and everyone is practicing in only cleats, shorts, and T-shirts. When you call this player out for their fictional skill sets, they become extremely verbally aggressive and act like they are a shoo-in, first-ballot Hall of Famer. Coaches tend to love their energy and effort but then always wonder where they went once the pads come on.

BEWARE OF THESE PRACTICE
COACH TYPES

MIND-READER COACH

The majority of NFL coaches have been in this business for a long time. They have had countless conversations with different players through the years and have had to repeatedly teach the same techniques and corrections again and again. The older the coach, the more impatient they tend to be when trying to get their point across.

The "mind-reader coach" will assume you know exactly what he is thinking most of the time and expect you to act accordingly. He may ask a question that has little to no context. He may ask you to perform a drill in practice that he hasn't fully explained. He may even ask you a question about one thing when he really means another. When you question him on his mistake he will yell at you as if you have no respect for him or his time. There is no solution to this situation. Try your best to do as he means and not as he says.

QUICK-LOOK CARD COACH

In practice, before every play, there will be a coach in charge of showing a "look card" to the scout team with a drawing of each player's responsibility. Occasionally, this coach will flash the card extremely quickly with no explanation other than a squiggling line depicting your role. Make sure you are focused and ready to quickly decipher your assignment; otherwise you'll be the a-hole either holding up practice because you need a second look or the brave S.O.B. who's going to guess what to do. Don't be either, but especially don't be the latter. You may get someone hurt or draw the fury of the coaching staff if you guess wrong.

MEETINGS

HOW TO HANDLE
FILM REVIEW

One of your daily job requirements is to have someone constantly pointing out your mistakes. A good coach will always challenge you to be your best, but some players are just too stubborn to accept criticism. Your coach may speak softly, curse, yell, throw things, berate, or simply act disappointed. All of these tactics are meant for the purpose of making you better. Check your ego at the door. Whether you agree with your coach's assessment or not, just say, "Yes, coach." Getting upset, arguing, making excuses, or walking out of the meeting does nothing but waste everyone's time and hurt your reputation with the team.

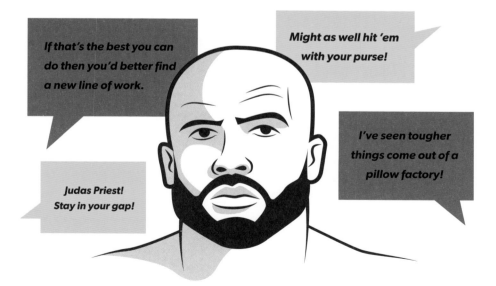

HOW TO
STAY AWAKE

Professional football meetings can be long and monotonous, especially late in the season. As a rookie, this will be the longest season you'll ever experience and at some point, you will hit the infamous "Rookie Wall." The first sign of the Rookie Wall will be heavy eyelids. It's okay to be tired, but sleeping in meetings sends the wrong message. Here are a couple of effective suggestions to fight drowsiness and stay focused.

NOTE:

Best excuse from a player called out by a coach for sleeping: "Naw, coach, I wasn't sleeping. I was just sayin' a quick prayer."

DRINK COFFEE
Be a grown-up and drink black coffee. Coffee with four sugars and four creams is hot chocolate. Children and Christmas carolers drink hot chocolate.

STAND UP
Awkward but much more respectable than falling asleep.

CHEW TOBACCO
Not recommended. Dangerous addiction, but effective. Con: oral cancer

CHEW SUNFLOWER SEEDS
Act like you've eaten them before. Don't crack them with your hands and don't smack with your mouth open. It's very loud and distracting.

THE IMPORTANCE OF
FILM STUDY

Your success is greatly dependent on your ability to study your opponent and identify their strengths and weaknesses. If you don't have great habits in studying game film, now's the time to learn. As always, watch how long-tenured pros go about studying their adversaries. They'll most likely always study every player as if it's their first time. Don't get overly nervous about notable players with impressive résumés and don't overlook players you've never heard of; they may surprise you. Watch as much film as you can, but please don't leave the door open to the film room in hopes that your coach will see you studying. (See the section on being the coach's pet.)

DÉJÀ VU
COACHING

While watching the film with your coach, you will begin to cringe as you get closer to seeing your bad play. Depending on your coach's style, you may get scorned in front of the group. Coach has made his point, you've learned your lesson, and now you can move on to the next opponent . . . or so you think. Except, at some point, you may have to watch that film again. Coaches can't remember all the plays they've corrected you on, so chances are you will be coached again, just as aggressively, on the same play later in the season. Hell, sometimes even later in your career!

GAME TIME

PREGAME MEAL

Whether you are home or away, your team will provide the same pregame spread four hours before every game. It will most likely include:

- OMELET STATION
- EGGS
- BACON
- SAUSAGE
- PANCAKES
- HASH BROWNS
- ASSORTED MUFFINS
  AND BREADS
- FRUIT
- GRILLED CHICKEN
- FILET MIGNON
- PASTA
- BROCCOLI
- GREEN BEANS
- BAKED POTATO
- COFFEE, TEAS, JUICE, WATER, AND SPORTS DRINKS

I shouldn't have had that ninth pancake . . . or the sausages . . .

Some players will take advantage of this all-you-can-eat buffet and do just that. The result is usually not good. The purpose of this meal is to fuel your body for the game, not put you into a coma. The smart players make bland choices with controlled portions. Don't experiment. Consult a nutritionist or ask a seasoned pro to help you figure out your pregame chow routine. You don't want to be on the field in the first quarter regretting that second helping of flapjacks.

BATHROOM LOGJAM

No matter how many times your teammates use the bathroom in their hotel room, they will always immediately head to the toilet stalls soon after arriving to the stadium. Not all visiting locker rooms are satisfactory. Many are small and provide only a few number of toilets for the team to use. When on the road, your team will schedule several different departure times for buses to take you to the stadium on game day. If you care about the condition in which you would like to find the toilet upon your arrival, then we suggest taking the early bus.

DO THE MATH

Fifty-three players with intense nerves, divided by three toilets, equals an endless traffic jam accompanied by a strong, unpleasant stench.

PRO TIPS

01 The game-day program that is given to every player in their locker is great bathroom material. By the time the game starts, the bathroom floor is littered with them.

02 If you come across a particularly gross-looking toilet, grab a towel from the showers and fold it around the top of the toilet seat. This can turn a bad situation into an enjoyable one.

If you happen to take the late bus and the bathroom line is too long, you could always use the head coach's private bathroom. But we highly recommend against that.

WILL CALL

You probably didn't heed our advice about game tickets and have just purchased thirty seats for family and friends. You're excited about putting on an NFL uniform and you want all your loved ones to be there to witness it. We were rookies once too—we get it. But now you have the distraction of having to organize and distribute these tickets before starting your game-day routine.

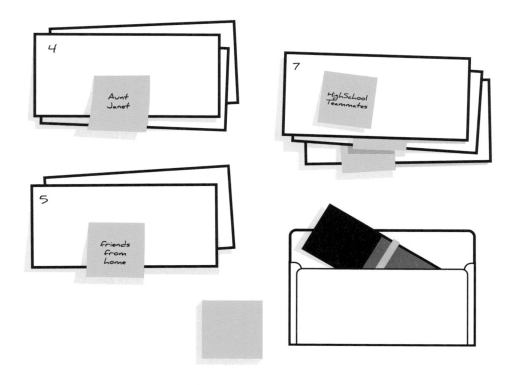

HOME GAME
INTRODUCTIONS

You worked your way into the starting lineup. It's a home game and you are standing in the tunnel waiting for your name to be called so you can run onto the field through the smoke and fire. This moment will say a lot about who you are as a player. Do you simply jog onto the field? Do you sprint? Do you attempt a dance routine? Helmet on or off? Would a simple point to the crowd suffice? Ask multiple players what they do when their name is called and they will likely all give you a slightly different answer. Whatever you do, have a plan. Don't be the idiot who leaves too early or too late. Pay attention to the entertainment director standing in the tunnel. They will tell you when to go out. Don't take too much time grandstanding . . . no one really cares too much about what you do. Remember that you are a rookie, not Ray Lewis, and your job requirement is to make plays on the field, not dance onto it.

SIDELINE
BATHROOM BREAK

Hydration is extremely important for every athlete, especially when playing in stadiums with warm weather climates. Now, what do you do when your bladder is asking for relief five minutes into the first quarter? Unfortunately, for some odd reason, the NFL doesn't provide easily accessible restrooms on the sidelines, so now you have to improvise. You can't leave for the locker room. What if there is a sudden change of possession? If you can't hold it until the half or after the game, here are a few quick effective fixes.

LOCKER-ROOM DASH

Typically, this is only acceptable if you are a backup. Be careful, though. You don't want to be mid-stream when the starter you back up goes down and you're nowhere to be found.

WALL OF BUDDIES

Gather a few players and/or equipment managers to shield you from the crowd. Find a water bottle, kneel down, and get your whiz on.

PEE YOUR PANTS

This only works if you're playing and soaking wet from sweat. Take a knee, empty the bladder, and rinse with a water bottle. Not recommended for white pants.

COACHING
EXPERIENCED PLAYERS

Everyone wants to feel like they are important and making a contribution, especially rookies who aren't playing. Great, that's fine, but do yourself and your teammates a favor and don't be a "player coach." A player coach is the guy with little to no experience in the pros trying to give starters advice on the sidelines during a game. Do us a favor: Shut up and go get the coach his clipboard.

> *I noticed you like to strike with your hands instead of grab? When I played at Eastern Midwest Tech, I used to . . .*

SUPPORT YOUR
TEAMMATES

You may not have won the starting job, or you did but got hurt. No one is saying you have to be happy about the situation, but, regardless of the circumstances, the guy playing your spot deserves your support. So smile and cheer 'im on . . . especially if you are a quarterback. The camera is always on you.

AFTER GAME
OPPONENT MINGLING

The game is over and both teams begin to trek toward the middle of the field to pay respect. You might know a former teammate or coach on the other side of the white lines or just want to quickly shake hands with a player you admire. It's always awkward to converse with another team after you beat them or just got beat. Listen for go-to lines like: "You guys are a hell of team" or "Enjoy watching you play" or "Did you come out healthy?" and "Good luck with the rest of the year, stay healthy!"

Remember, your time mingling on the field will be determined by the outcome of the game. Keep your chitchat, pictures, and jersey exchanging brief. Make sure to gauge when other players start to head in. You don't want to be the one who returns to the locker room in the middle of the head coach's speech.

TRASH TALKING

You can't have one of the most violent arenas in all of sports without the most offensive and obnoxious banter. If you get the chance to play on Sundays, you'll catch everything from outbursts of profanity to the most vulgar personal attacks you've ever heard.

If you are not a trash-talker, don't start now. There are too many players who have become masters at the art of verbal warfare. Tune it out and focus on the next play. The objective of a trash-talker is to either distract you or psych themselves into being tougher than they really are.

If talking trash is part of your game, that's fine, but don't be a distraction to yourself or your teammates. If your group is in the huddle trying to call a play but you're dialoguing with another player like a Bond villain . . . that's a problem. Shut up and get in the huddle. The play clock doesn't wait for you to finish exchanging insults. Also, you'd better not get a penalty for taking it too far, because then you may have to answer to a coach who has offensive words of his own.

Remember, empty cans make the loudest noise. So save your energy for the game. Do your talking with your play and don't say anything you may regret. There are microphones everywhere.

HOW TO
ARGUE WITH REFEREES

Everyone has their own feelings and opinions about referees. They are the smartest, greatest bunch when a call goes your team's way . . . and the most vile, corrupt scumbags on earth when a call goes against you. However much ill-will you feel toward them, making enemies will not help you or your team. Referees are humans; they make mistakes. They have to look for a million things at once. You may not be able to convince them to overturn a bad call, but here are a few tips to help them notice the things they are overlooking.

NO YELLING OR CURSING
Screaming vulgar obscenities does nothing but shut them off to you. You can get your point across in a respectful way without being a jerk.

KNOW THEIR NAMES

Knowing an official's name, especially in the small fraternity of the league, shows the respect you have for them and the game.

Hey, you. The guy is holding me all day!

BUILD A RAPPORT

The longer you play, the more you can get to know these enforcers of the rules. Guess what? Most of them are really good people trying to be the best at their craft. Establishing a relationship doesn't mean calls are going to start going your way, but at least it gives you an opportunity to have them hear you out.

Hey, Jeff. Appreciate the warning, but if you call a penalty on me for that, I'm not sending you a Christmas card.

ONE SNAP
AND CLEAR

There's an old saying that big-time players make big-time plays in big-time games. Well, unfortunately, big-time players also make big-time mistakes. The difference between the great ones and the ones who quickly fade from the league? The great ones know how to identify what went wrong, learn from it, make the correction, and never think about it again. The ones who feel sorry for themselves develop fears of repeating mistakes and struggle to move on. Games are long. Everyone makes mistakes, but the quicker you can learn and get over it, the sooner you can focus on the next play and redeem yourself.

NOTE:

Mistakes in the game are one thing, but embarrassing plays that live in infamy can be tougher to recover from. Whether you run the ball into the wrong end zone or fumble on your teammate's gluteus maximus, all you can do is move forward and hopefully make enough good plays to overshadow the bad.

RESPECT
FOR THE GAME

Football is an intense sport. This game of high-speed collisions requires you to make quick decisions while playing as physically as possible. That being said, the rules of the game can sometimes hinder you from making swift decisions that are both effective and legal. While we don't always agree with some of the rules, the NFL is intent on making the game as safe and fair as possible. Respect the rules and respect your colleagues. You're not the only one playing hard to stay employed. Getting beat on the field doesn't give you the right to retaliate. If you are not good enough to do your job, then practice harder and study more film.

The game celebrates great catches, hits, and throws, not trips, holds, and cheap shots. So don't step on a guy's hand as you walk away from a pile or give the opposing sideline the bird, because not only is it dishonorable, but there are cameras everywhere!

OCCUPATIONAL HAZARDS

FOOTBALL IS
DANGEROUS

It's no secret that football is a hazardous profession. This sport is also immensely popular, which means it's not going to cease to exist anytime soon. If you are successful, it can be a very rewarding experience, both financially and emotionally. If you are concerned about the dangers and long-term effects the game may present, then you should probably pursue another line of work. No one is forcing you to play football. Whatever you decide, the game will go on with or without you.

INJURY SYSTEM CHECK
TOUGH METER

Understand something: you get paid a lot of money to play football. The fans, the organization, and most importantly, your teammates all expect you to be out there on the field. Injuries are part of the game, but you have to know the difference between being hurt and being injured. Jammed fingers, rolled ankles, sprained wrists, turf toes, broken noses, bone bruises, hyperextension, and countless other nicks and aches. Hurt, not injured. Some of these things, if not all of them, will happen to you at one point or another in your career. The quicker you can distinguish between temporary discomfort and incapacity, the more valuable you'll be to the organization, your team, and yourself.

A wise trainer once said, "Motion is lotion." Although it may be painful, pushing through an ailment can have a self-correcting effect that keeps you on the field. "Rubbing some dirt on it" may even help you forget what was bothering you in the first place. So, unless you've completely torn a ligament, broken a bone, or have a headache accompanied by confusion, there is no reason you shouldn't be out on the field helping your team try to win. Then again . . . plenty of the greats have played through worse.

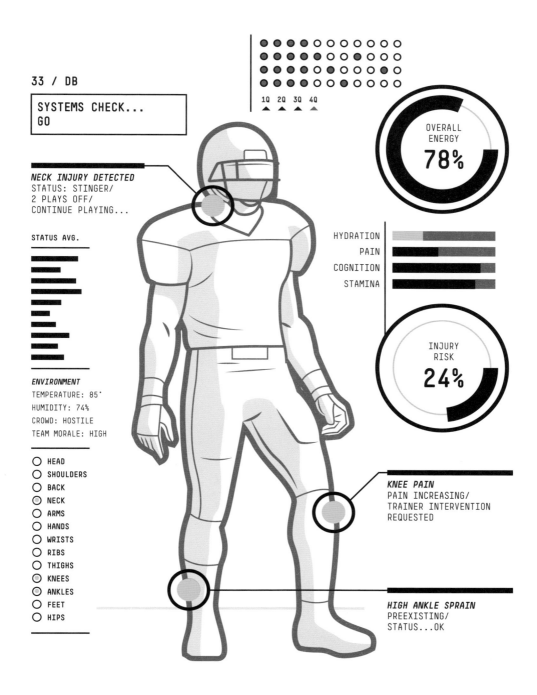

33 / DB

SYSTEMS CHECK...
GO

1Q 2Q 3Q 4Q

NECK INJURY DETECTED
STATUS: STINGER/
2 PLAYS OFF/
CONTINUE PLAYING...

STATUS AVG.

ENVIRONMENT
TEMPERATURE: 85°
HUMIDITY: 74%
CROWD: HOSTILE
TEAM MORALE: HIGH

- ○ HEAD
- ○ SHOULDERS
- ○ BACK
- ◎ NECK
- ○ ARMS
- ○ HANDS
- ○ WRISTS
- ○ RIBS
- ○ THIGHS
- ◎ KNEES
- ◎ ANKLES
- ○ FEET
- ○ HIPS

OVERALL
ENERGY
78%

HYDRATION
PAIN
COGNITION
STAMINA

INJURY
RISK
24%

KNEE PAIN
PAIN INCREASING/
TRAINER INTERVENTION
REQUESTED

HIGH ANKLE SPRAIN
PREEXISTING/
STATUS...OK

HIGH FIVES
ELBOW PROTECTION

When a player's name is announced during pregame introductions he runs onto the field greeted by cheers. Next, he races through a human tunnel made up of teammates on either side. If you are part of this high-fiving wall of testosterone, then you should be cautious of putting your arm in a vulnerable position. Your elbow can only bend so far, and some of your teammates will run through slapping your hand at different speeds. This is not a joke. If your elbow gets hyperextended from an excessively aggressive, supersonic hand-slapper, it could affect your game. That being said, you don't want to be the guy who doesn't embrace your teammates as they take the field.

Here's a quick solution that protects your elbow and still allows you to be a good team-mate. Put out the hand opposite of the running lane. This puts your arm in a position that bends with maximum give.

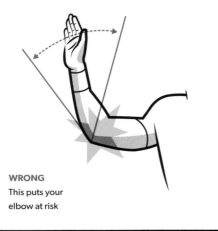

WRONG
This puts your
elbow at risk

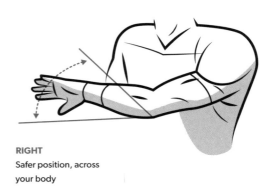

RIGHT
Safer position, across
your body

TAKING
PERSONAL TIME

THIS TEAM HAS WORKED

19,820 **DAYS**

WITHOUT TIME LOST
TO YOUR PERSONAL LIFE

SICK DAYS

There is no such thing as calling in sick in pro football. Having the flu, a stomachache, or a sick family member who needs caretaking will not get you a day off work. Your team has invested a lot of money in you and you're expected to be there every day. If you do wake up feeling sick, get to the training room as quickly as possible so the trainers can assess your status. They can provide you with an IV, medicine, or a visit with the doctor. The only circumstance you would be sent home is if the team doctor feared you might make others on the team ill. So, if you really need a day off, you better give a performance worthy of an Academy Award.

HAVING A BABY

You've got a baby on the way? Congratulations! News flash, the NFL doesn't care, especially if it means you might miss a game. There's no easy answer or advice. This is a serious decision that requires a lot of thought. Obviously, life happens and you can't always schedule having a baby. Still, good luck receiving the blessing of the organization for you to miss a game so you can be present for your child's birth.

TAKE CONTROL OF
YOUR REHAB

Injuries are commonplace in the NFL. Being injured can be a difficult circumstance. There's a helplessness about it, and coaches and teammates will often try to guilt you into returning sooner than you are ready. This is because many players don't know the difference between being hurt and being injured. If you are truly injured, then you have to be diligent and take ownership of your rehab. Don't enter the training room only to lie on a table waiting for someone to appear and cater to your every need. Ask questions, be proactive, and get your ass back on the field. You don't want to be the next Wally Pipp. You know, the Yankees' first baseman who sat out one game with a headache only to be replaced by the legendary Lou Gehrig.

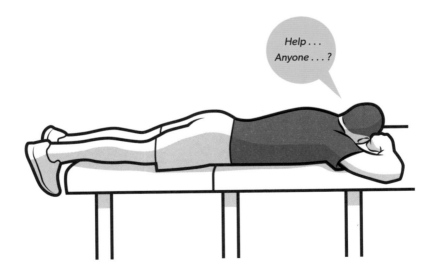

Help . . .
Anyone . . . ?

GETTING CUT:
STAYING IN SHAPE

Most professional football players will be cut at some point in their career. It can be very frustrating and disheartening when you are released, and you might feel like drowning your sorrows on the couch with copious amounts of fast food and video games. But if you hope to keep playing, get off the couch and head to the gym while you are waiting for your next opportunity. When a team decides to bring you in for a workout or sign you to the roster, you will be on a plane, sometimes within hours of getting a call. Showing up out of shape will get you a return flight home.

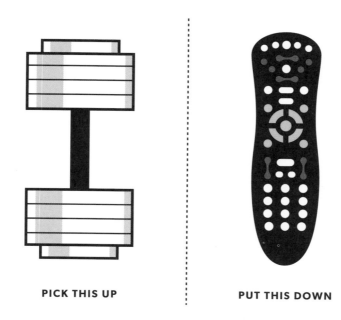

PICK THIS UP   **PUT THIS DOWN**

AVOIDING
RISKY CELEBRATIONS

Great, you scored a touchdown, sacked the quarterback, made a great block . . . whoop-dee-do, you did your job. Don't act like you are the first person to make a play. Besides, your average fan appreciates the humble player anyway. However, you are a rookie, and humility may not be your style. If you make a big play and decide to celebrate, be aware that there may be consequences. First of all, there's the chance you can get yourself a stupid penalty. Second, opponents love to put a bull's-eye on the chest of an arrogant player. Last, history has shown that excessive celebrations can sometimes lead to serious injury. Ask yourself this question: "Do I really want to be known for tearing my ACL after cartwheeling through the endzone?"

PREMATURE CELEBRATION
In your excitement about getting to the house, make sure you remember the little things, like having the ball in your hands when you break the plane.

BUTT HEAD

That feeling? That's the adrenaline rush of scoring in the big leagues. That over there? That's a wall. Don't hit it with your head.

DANGEROUS RICOCHET

If you're going to thread the needle with a powerful spike, the angle of your trajectory better be perfect.

ARMS WIDE OPEN

You're big, you're mean, you're powerful, and you just got the sack. You also just tore your ACL and have six to nine months of rehab to look forward to.

NOTE: This will be the look on your head coach's face when you get to the sideline after a dumb penalty because you just had to do the greatest celebration of all time.

SECTION 10

MAINTENANCE

PHARMACY

The game will take a toll on your body, but, as an NFL player, your athletic trainers can provide you access to some of the greatest health professionals in the world. Pain and sickness are inevitable. If you must take medicine or prescribed anti-inflammatories, use only as directed by your team doctor. As for painkillers, they will be given out on an extremely limited basis, if at all. Gone are the days when prescriptions were passed around without checks and balances. If you're ever uncomfortable or unsure of what you're being prescribed, then try being a grown-up and do your own research. Take responsibility for what you put into your body.

ADVICE: Instead of playing *NBA 2K* all evening, peruse the internet for information on what you are being offered. Educate yourself on the pros and cons of everything you take.

HOW TO APPLY
WRIST TAPE

If you don't know how to tape your own wrists by now, it proves just how spoiled and pampered you were at your college. You are a rookie and that already puts you last in line for ankle taping. Your wrists are even further down on the priority list. Bottom line, it's time to start taping yourself. Watch the vets who play your position and study their techniques. They've spent years perfecting it, so learn from their experience. In the meantime, here is a quick guide to a few standard tape techniques to get you started.

MATERIALS NEEDED:

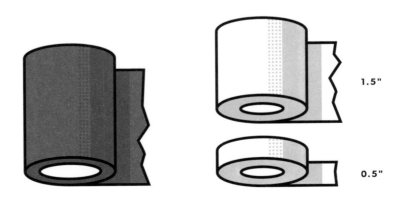

1.5"

0.5"

MOST FREQUENT TAPE TECHNIQUES: HAND/WRIST

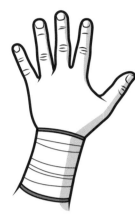

THE STANDARD

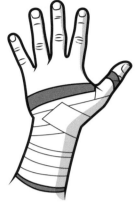

WRIST AND THUMB

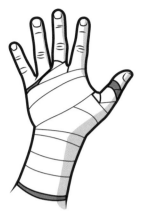

THE BOXER

MOST FREQUENT TAPE TECHNIQUES: FINGERS

FIGURE EIGHT

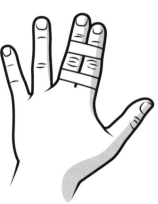

THE BUDDY SYSTEM

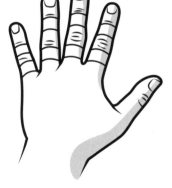

FINGER MAN

WARNING!
If your fingers become tingly or turn blue or purple, the tape is too tight. Remove and retape.

TAKING
SUPPLEMENTS

There's no doubt that there are players in this league who have enhanced their abilities and recovery by taking performance-enhancing drugs. For the vast majority of us who have decided to follow the rules, we rely on vitamins and supplements to improve our strength and health. Still, unless you're a world-renowned biochemist, navigating through the thousands of supplement companies trying to find products that are free of banned substances can be extremely daunting.

Your safest bet is to use products that are certified by the league. Also, your team will provide resources to help you determine what's safe. Beware, even if your team and the league verify that the ingredients listed on a product contain no substances in violation of the NFL's prohibited-substance policy, they will still tell you: **You and you alone are responsible for what goes into your body.** So take at your own risk.

PREMIUM
TURBO
MUSCLES

TRUST US, PLEASE

XL
DUDE

TOTALLY SAFE

RIP'D

PROTEIN MUSCLE
BUILDER

PERFORM
X

WEIGHT MANAGEMENT

Scouts, coaches, and general managers are *obsessed* with how much a player weighs. Ultimately, you are judged by how you play, but the powers that be can't resist making up an arbitrary weight they think you should maintain. If you find yourself at the weekly weigh-in either too light or too heavy for your required weight, here are some proven veteran techniques to help you get by.

TOO LIGHT

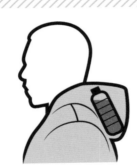

HIDDEN WEIGHT
Place an unnoticed water bottle in your hand or somewhere on your body.

NO-GO
Don't go to the bathroom before your weigh-in.

PACK IT IN
Eat a large meal and lots of liquids before the next day's weigh-in.

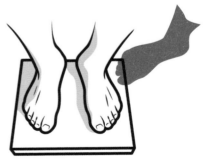

GRAVITY HELPER
Have a sneaky friend get a foot on the scale to help add some weight.

GET STEAMED
Hit the steam room and sweat off
some extra weight.

SPITTING
Chew lots of gum and do lots of
spitting. Gross but effective.

LAXATIVES
Invest in a good laxative.
Use as needed.

JUST SAY NO
The morning of the weigh-in,
say no to breakfast.

MORNING SWEAT
Get in one last early morning circuit and
shed a few pounds before the weigh-in.

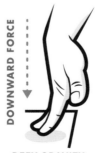

DOWNWARD FORCE

DEFY GRAVITY
Discretely find something to push on
and lift a little weight off the scale.

COMMON
TREATMENTS

You sacrifice your health in order to make money. Now it's time to spend that money in order to recuperate. It's a bit amusing when you think about it that way, but this is what we all signed up for. Football players will try anything that might prolong or help their careers. Here are a few common treatments. Try 'em all, see what works for you, or don't take care of your body, get hurt all the time, and act confused when you do.

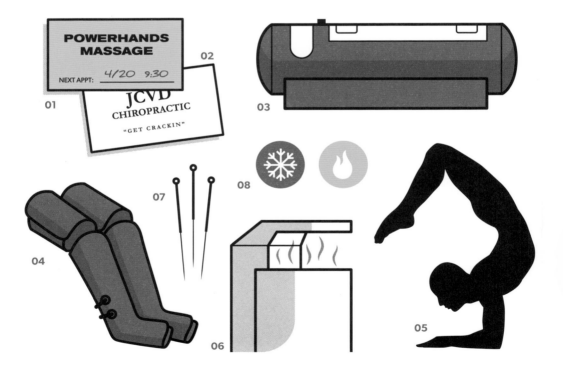

POWERHANDS MASSAGE

NEXT APPT: 4/20 9:30

01

JCVD CHIROPRACTIC

"GET CRACKIN"

02

03

07

08

04

06

05

01 MASSAGE

Who doesn't love a full body massage? Sometimes, though, a massage can leave you as sore as a tough workout. Our advice would be to try not to schedule one too close to a game.

02 CHIROPRACTOR

This is a therapy that has just as many opponents as advocates. Maybe because there is such a thing as a dangerously bad chiropractor. So make sure you work with someone who knows what they are doing. You don't want someone with little experience snapping your neck like in a Jean-Claude Van Damme movie.

03 HYPERBARIC CHAMBER

This atmospheric-pressure-controlled body tube of pure oxygen is used for a variety of serious sicknesses, infections, and injuries. Jocks use it to enhance their body's "natural healing process." In any case, it's a great place to nap.

04 AIR COMPRESSION LEG WRAPS

These fancy leggings supposedly help improve circulation and reduce swelling. These are great if your legs feel heavy after a long practice or if you want to simulate what it would feel like to have an anaconda squeeze your thighs.

05 YOGA

You think football is hard? Try a one-handed tree pose or a scorpion pose variation. This ancient discipline is great for building strength and flexibility.

06 CRYOTHERAPY CHAMBER

Step into this chilly chamber of freezing liquid nitrogen for a couple of minutes and cut your recovery time from 72 to 24 hours . . . or so they claim.

07 ACUPUNCTURE

If you're afraid of needles, this might not be the therapy for you. Many players swear by acupuncture; others think it has a placebo affect. Regardless, many use it and it's been around a few thousand years . . . must be something to it.

08 CONTRAST HYDROTHERAPY

Sounds fancy, right? It's basically just going back and forth between immersing yourself in a hot water tub and a cold water tub. The idea is that the extreme changes in temperatures cause your body to send blood faster to sore or injured areas to help speed recovery. There are plenty of studies for and against it. Whether it works or not, most players couldn't live without it.

TOC — TREATMENT OF CONVENIENCE

Got time to kill in between meetings? Need to catch up on a few emails? How about getting some extra sleep? If you sleep in the locker room or sit and scroll through your phone, you might send the coach the wrong impression. Instead, head to the training room and ask a trainer to give you treatment on something that allows you to just lie there. Maybe your ankle is "sore" or your calf is "tight." It's a jerk move to the trainer, but everyone is guilty of it.

MEDIA

The media is your conduit to the world of sports fans. There are great sports writers and interviewers who put a lot of work and thought into what they write and report. Unfortunately, there are also many who publish sensationalized, fabricated rubbish. You may not want to speak with them, but you're contractually obligated to meet with all members of the media. Be respectful, but stay guarded. You can't control the questions, but you can always control your answers.

NUDE & INTERVIEWED

Privacy is a thing of the past, and, many times throughout the week, media is granted access to the locker room. Whether you like it or not, both male and female members of the media will be present, usually right around the time you need to shower. Cameras roll right away, so don't be afraid to ask if you may have a moment to cover up. Bottom line . . . cover up your bottom line.

GETTING THE PERFECT
TEAM PICTURE

Your team picture is going to be pulled up for a plethora of reasons—starting lineup, game-time programs, media outlets. It's going to be the same picture used for the positive and negative news. Do yourself a favor and look presentable. If you don't want people to think you're an idiot, then don't look like one in your team picture.

TOO SCARY

"Sources close with team say they are still trying to decide if player's off-field issues are true."

TOO CHEESY

"Ownership questions Rookie Offensive Tackle's commitment to the game."

JUST RIGHT

Note the "you can trust me" smile and the confident, straightforward stance.

ANSWERS

It's always easy to speak with the media after a good performance or win. Your real test comes when you have to answer for a bad day at the office. Control your emotions, take responsibility for your performance, and answer the questions . . . even the dumb ones.

TYPICAL MEDIA GUY QUESTION: "It looked like you really struggled today against that All-Pro Defensive End. Stat sheets show you giving up three sacks. How does that feel?"

WHAT YOU WANT TO SAY:

"How does it feel? HOW DOES IT FEEL?! It feels great, moron! I really enjoyed watching that jerk who beat me for those sacks dance and shake his ass celebrating. I'll probably get cut after this season because of today! How come no one's mentioning how deep the quarterback was?! And where was the running back to help me? Make sure you ask the coordinator why I couldn't get more quick passes!"

WHAT YOU SHOULD SAY:

"I had a tough day against a quality opponent. I need to work harder this week to get better. I've got another tough test next week."

This answer is boring, but at least you won't end up on *SportsCenter* or alienate your coaches and teammates.

THE REPHRASE
INTERVIEW

From puff pieces to scandals, the media is in the business of selling stories. Warranted or not, you may not like a certain reporter because of what they reported about you or your team, but you have to respect how hard of a task they have in finding new and interesting story lines daily.

For the most part, many reporters have already decided what story they want to tell and are only interviewing you to find quotes for it. Even if you want no part in a particular story and you deflect, be on the lookout for the rephrase game. Reporters are great at asking the same question disguised in different ways.

Be gracious and keep it civil. And, should you ever decide to challenge a member of the media, consider what legendary basketball owner Jerry Buss once famously said: "Never get in pissing matches with people who buy ink by the barrel."

"It seems like you're limping. Are you hurt?"	→	"I noticed during the game your teammate fell on your leg. Is that when you got hurt?"	→	"Coach didn't say anything about an injury for you during his press conference. Does that mean you're healthy?"

GIVING OUT YOUR
PHONE NUMBER

The media is neither your enemy nor your friend. The league allots plenty of time for the local beat writers to ask you questions. Don't give your phone number to them. They will abuse your free time by constantly soliciting you for insider information.

TEXTS FROM REPORTER MATT

> Hey bud, how's your family?

> Good thanks

> Getting to play much golf?

> Not really

> Hear anything about how long our running back might be out?

> Got any weekend plans?

> Gotta run

> What's the injury report going into the bye?

SECTION 12

TEAM PERSONNEL

THE REALITY OF YOUR
ROOKIE CLASS

It's an incredible accomplishment and feeling when you get the call to compete for a job with an NFL franchise. The first people you'll meet are the other rookies in your class, both drafted and free agents. There's a bond you immediately share. Unfortunately, that bond is short-lived and you will soon experience the anxiety and gloom of watching friends you've made in a short time be told to pack their things and be on their way. It may happen in the first week or slowly over a few years. You might be the last of your class or the first to go. It's a sad reality that we *all* must face.

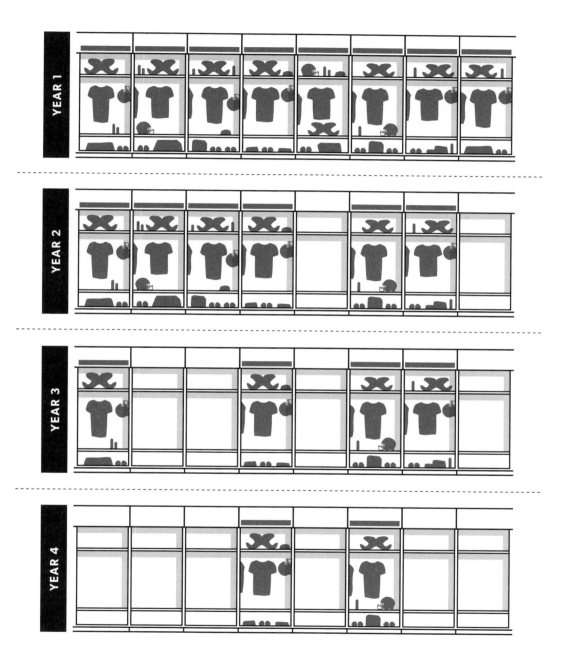

YEAR 1

YEAR 2

YEAR 3

YEAR 4

FRONT OFFICE

In your first season as a pro, you will probably have limited interaction with the personnel "upstairs." Scouts or the general manager might ask you about a former college teammate or give you some words of encouragement, but that will probably be the extent of it. Be cordial since these are likely the people making final decisions on the roster. That being said, having an inside joke with the GM doesn't protect you from cut day. So be discreet — teammates will quickly label you a brownnoser if you spend too much time kissing up to members of the front office.

ATHLETIC TRAINING STAFF

Athletic trainers spend long, tedious hours helping you prevent injuries and putting you back together. From taping ankles to rubbing hamstrings, the common cold to season-ending surgeries, team athletic trainers are the catalyst for any and all issues concerning your health on and off the field. They are also part of the evaluation in selecting the roster.

Athletic trainers have a complicated job in that they have to walk a fine line between protecting the best interest of the team and that of the player. Some athletic trainers do right by both, while others tend to lean one way or the other. The point is, they carry a lot of weight in the fate of your employment with the team.

It's *not* hard to be in an athletic trainer's good graces. All they require of you is to be attentive and on time for treatment and doctor appointments, respect their staff, and, especially, respect their training room. The training room is a special place where players gather to make jokes, tell stories, have friendly debates, and heal.

EQUIPMENT STAFF

Contrary to popular belief, these guys do more than inflate and deflate footballs on game day. The equipment staff work some of the longest days of anyone in the organization. They fit you for your gear, pass out sweats when it's cold, and make sure you have the right shoes for any condition. They also pack and unpack the gear for road games, set up for practice, and keep the locker room from smelling musty—and they rarely complain. Without them, it would be hard to get anything done.

They are also not your personal assistants or an athletic apparel store. You may notice older players receive preferential treatment. That's because they've built the relationship over the years and/or have earned the right. As a rookie, you get what you get. So make sure you treat the equipment staff with the respect they deserve.

ADVICE: It is customary to give the lower-level equipment personnel a tip at the end of the year as a show of your appreciation for their hard work. If you are pondering being cheap, remember that they've worked long hours picking up your filthy equipment and disgustingly sweaty jocks.

OWNER

Some owners are incredibly involved with their franchise, while others allow those they've hired to run the show. Depending on which team you're on, you may see the owner around all the time or never. When they do come around, unless you're the star quarterback or one of the longest-tenured players on the team, the owner has no inclination to get to know you. So leave the owner be and forget any fantasies you may have of joining him on his private plane for a quick trip to the Hamptons. Kissing up to the front office will label you a brownnoser. Kissing up to the owner? Now that's a Royal Brownnoser!

LIFE IN THE BIG LEAGUES

KNOW YOUR
FANS

Fans are the lifeblood of the National Football League. They spend their time and hard-earned money to support their favorite teams. Fans buy tickets, jerseys, and merchandise, which in turn allows you to earn the nice salary that you will make as a professional football player. Without them, there would be no robust television contracts or sold-out, state-of-the-art stadiums. That being said, there are varying levels of fandom, from the adorable little kids wearing your jersey to the social-media troll who hatefully tweets at you after every loss.

EBAY FAN

This "fan" is normally a middle-aged, overweight male. He will be easy to spot because he will be holding numerous full-sized helmets that he aggressively shoves in your face to have you sign. Chances are he will also be in possession of a camera to "discreetly" take your picture while you are signing so he can prove the authenticity of the signatures once the helmets make their way to eBay. It is perfectly acceptable to avoid this "fan" once they have been properly identified.

KIDS

These are the absolute best fans. They just want an autograph on a piece of notebook paper or a picture with you so they can go show it off to their little buddies at school. Go out of your way to accommodate these fans.

SOCIAL-MEDIA TROLL

The veil of anonymity makes the social-media troll feel extra tough. This fan will post hateful comments about you, your team, and, sometimes, even your family, especially after a tough loss. *Never* respond to this fan. You will not win.

DINNER INTERRUPTER

Fans will frequently approach you at restaurants for a picture or autograph, especially when you are eating with teammates, making you easily identifiable as a member of the home team. This can be frustrating when you are actively eating, and it is absolutely acceptable to ask them politely to come back once you are through with your meal.

CREEPY FAN

The creepy fan has an abundance of free time that they devote solely to their team. This fan stands outside of practice daily just to greet you as you walk by before and after practice. They will know a disturbing amount of information about your personal life, including but not limited to the names of your spouse and kids or your birthday. The creepy fan means well and is extremely devoted, so be friendly but not overengaging.

FRUSTRATED FAN

The frustrated fan is a version of the loyal fan, but one who takes the losses a little harder. They might lash out and yell, "You suck!" or "You couldn't play dead," but they soon regret their outburst, feel silly, and realize that they still love the home team. It's tolerable to give them a look that says, "You're an a-hole!," but keep moving and don't respond.

LOYAL FAN

The loyal fan loves his or her team almost to a fault. This fan is equally supportive through the twelve-win season and the two-win season. This fan is scarce, but highly valued. Once you have identified the loyal fan, show your appreciation to this rare species.

THE FRONT-RUNNER

This fan couldn't care less about the team until you reach a minimum of ten wins and have clinched a spot in the playoffs. Once you have reached their threshold for success, they love you. Beware, the front-runner will kick you to the curb as soon as there is any sign of adversity.

CASUAL

This fan has general knowledge about his or her team and likely owns a T-shirt or hat to show support for the team. He or she attends the occasional home game when free tickets are available. They hope for the best but don't get overly worked up if things don't go well for the home team.

AWAY-GAME HECKLER FANS

The pro stadium environment is verbally hostile, so you better have thick skin coming from your family-friendly college town games. These fans are usually right behind your team's benches and most of them are experienced verbal bullies with years of season-ticket-holding practice. While you are studying your opponent for the game on Sunday, these savvy trash-talkers are studying anything and everything they can find on the internet about your personal life. Their objectives are simple: Get your attention, make you mad, and keep you focused on them rather than the game. They may even hope to get your teammates to laugh at your expense. Pro tip: Smile. Showing them you're annoyed only fuels their fire.

FANTASY FOOTBALL FANS

Millions of people play fantasy football, but hardcore fantasy football fans are a special breed. These fans only care about individual player production. They have no sense of team or winning; they're obsessed with what kind of stats you had for a given game. Regardless of your health status or role for that week, these fans feel entitled to production since they drafted you in their fantasy league. Whether at the grocery store, a restaurant with your family, or on social media, if you didn't give them the points they needed for that week, they'll give you a piece of their mind.

Fantasy Football League Smack Talk Board:

Today, 6:45 PM

Red Hot Julius Peppers	How'd that receiver you pick up last week work out for you?

Today, 7:46 PM

Brady Gaga	He comes into our restaurant once a week. I'm dropping a mucus ball in that clown's minestrone for every dropped pass he had against Chicago!

HOW TO
FIND YOUR SEAT

You did the right thing and arrived early to your first team meeting to find the perfect seat and maybe to impress the coach. Unbeknownst to you, you sat in the seat of an eight-year veteran kicker who just gave you the boot. Now you're looking to find a seat seconds before the meeting starts.

Most players call dibs on a seat. Whether it's in a meeting room, on the team bus, or on a plane, a player's permanent seat helps establish routine and even status. Our advice? Ask an older player or coach which seats are available. They are usually willing to help; well, unless they steer you wrong for their own entertainment and just want to see you scramble. But have no fear, we've provided the following useful sample seating charts to help you navigate these uncertain waters.

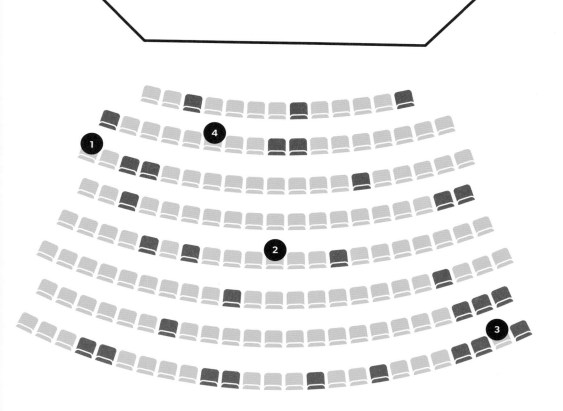

TEAM MEETING ROOM *(75 Seat Capacity)*

AVAILABLE

RESERVED

SEATS TO AVOID

1. Twenty-six-year coach who hates players who chew sunflower seeds in meetings
2. All-Pro loud-mouth D-tackle
3. Grumpy nine-year center
4. Second-year "Hall of Fame" running back (in his own mind)

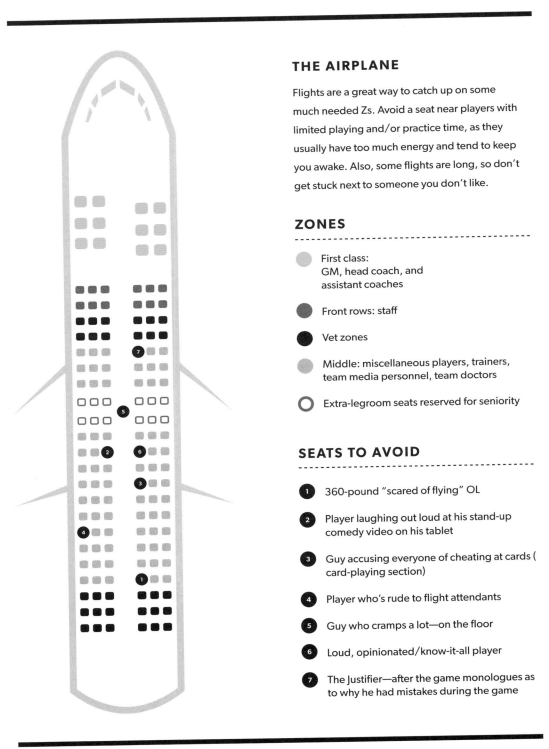

THE AIRPLANE

Flights are a great way to catch up on some much needed Zs. Avoid a seat near players with limited playing and/or practice time, as they usually have too much energy and tend to keep you awake. Also, some flights are long, so don't get stuck next to someone you don't like.

ZONES

First class:
GM, head coach, and
assistant coaches

Front rows: staff

Vet zones

Middle: miscellaneous players, trainers,
team media personnel, team doctors

Extra-legroom seats reserved for seniority

SEATS TO AVOID

1   360-pound "scared of flying" OL

2   Player laughing out loud at his stand-up
comedy video on his tablet

3   Guy accusing everyone of cheating at cards (
card-playing section)

4   Player who's rude to flight attendants

5   Guy who cramps a lot—on the floor

6   Loud, opinionated/know-it-all player

7   The Justifier—after the game monologues as
to why he had mistakes during the game

THE TEAM BUS

Coaches usually sit toward the front of the bus. So the further back you can sit, the more freedom you can have with your conversations. If the bus looks full and you have to double up with someone, try to find a seat next to the smallest rookie you can spot.

ZONES

 Coaches

● Vet zone

● Middle: Miscellaneous players, trainers, team media personnel, team doctors

SEATS TO AVOID

 Loud, always on his phone player

❷ Recluse, headphones player

❸ Staff member/snitch—listens in on players' conversations and reports to coach

 The Justifier—after the game monologues as to why he had mistakes during the game.

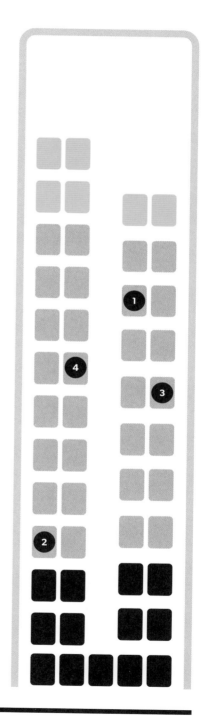

TEAM DINING
TABLE UPGRADE

Mealtime in the NFL provides a great opportunity for fellowship with your teammates. It's typically the only time you have all day to sit and relax, but selecting a table in the cafeteria is not so simple. You must be aware of the possibility of being stuck with a boring or annoying tablemate. If, by your own fault, you find yourself part of a poor table population, then you're stuck. Unless you pull a move called "The Upgrade."

The Upgrade is simply identifying a table you would rather sit at and leaving those poor souls behind for that "better" table. It's a move that says, "I'd sit with you if there were no other options, but that table is better so I'm outta here!" It's a bush league move but at least it's honest.

Keep in mind that the Upgrade can also happen to you. If it does . . . take a good, hard look in the mirror and try to figure out why a teammate couldn't stomach sitting with you for a twenty-minute meal.

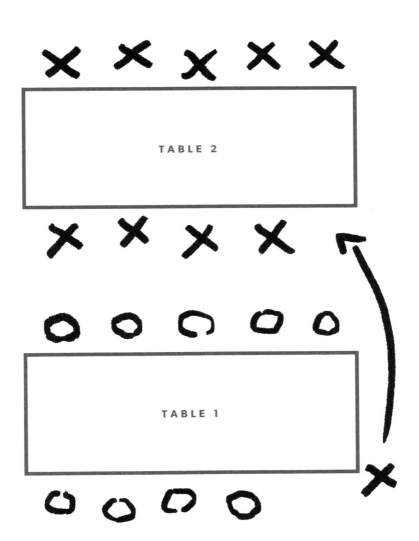

POWER RIGHT SWEEP
LEAVE BORING TABLE
4 BETTER TABLE
ON QUICK COUNT

TIPS ON
EQUIPMENT

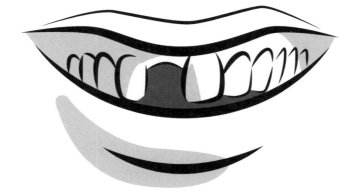

MOUTHPIECE

Do you like losing your teeth? How about receiving concussions? If the answer is no to both, then do yourself a favor and get a custom mouthpiece. For whatever reason, a lot of players don't have them. They take little time out of your day to concoct with a team dentist, and guess what? The team pays for them!

KNEE BRACE

Some of you might have been obligated to wear custom protective knee braces in college. They were annoying to put on, uncomfortable, and usually stank because, let's be honest, you never washed them. Numerous rookies bring their braces from college and usually find out pretty quickly that they can't keep up with the speed at the next level. Advice? Unless you have a preexisting condition that requires them for safety . . . ditch 'em. Chances are, your restrictive Forest Gump leg braces will hinder you more than protect you. And at this level? You need every advantage you can get.

DEALING WITH YOUR
HOTEL ROOMMATE

Most teams will institute a roommate policy at the team hotel for younger players. You will be assigned a roommate for the season. This relationship is important because getting good sleep the night before the game is incredibly important. Caution, a good roommate will be harder to find than you think. Look out for the following types:

HURRICANE ROOMMATE
First to use the bathroom, leaving you a scattered mess of used towels, dirty laundry, shaved hairs, and the most indescribable stench from the toilet bowl.

HOST WITH THE MOST
Without your consent, your sleeping quarters just got turned into the official card-playing room for half the team.

UNLIMITED TALK PLAN
Loudly talking on his phone late into the night as if you aren't even in the room.

SURROUND SOUND
Keeps the television volume on max capacity at all times.

SCARED OF THE DARK
Why are there so many lights on all the time?

ROOM SERVICE ROULETTE
Orders food for one but for some reason you split the bill.

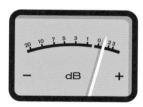

SLEEP APNEA
Elephants don't make that much noise.

XXX
Adult-content addict enjoys perusing the after-hours channels.

CHEMICAL WARFARE
You need a gas mask for the poisonous fumes leaching from your roomie.

SELF-TALKING HYPE MAN
Constantly telling you all about what he's going to do the next day.

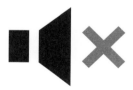

QUIET AND SHY
You begin to wonder if your roommate can speak?

THE SCALES
OF TOLERANCE

Your ultimate value in the pros is wrapped up in how well you play the game of football. That being said, fans tune in not only for the excitement and drama an NFL season holds but also to watch the polarizing personalities.

You can be a horrid human being and still have a roster spot on a team because of your tremendous gifts as an athlete. However, if the weight of your jackass-ness is greater than your ability to catch, run, tackle, block, etc. . . . you'll be shown the door.

Everything you do is being evaluated, including the way you treat people and how you work with others. Almost everyone gets cut at some point. You can expedite that process by playing poorly or being an exceedingly terrible person, or both.

CHARITABLE DONATION

GAME WINNING TD

EMOTIONAL TEAM SPEECH ABOUT LOVE FOR TEAMMATES

MISSED BLOCKS

PUSHED FAN

MISSED MEETING

PUNCHED TEAMMATE

DROPPED PASSES

CALLED OUT TEAMMATES ON TV

DUI

DID NOT FINISH GAME

PERSONAL FOULS

RAN WRONG PLAY

BROKE DRESS CODE

CURSED OUT COACH

DRUG TESTING

**THE COMMON VARIETY
DRUG TESTER**

You've been subject to drug testing in one form or another during your high school or college career, but probably not as frequently as you will now be tested. Every player will be tested twice during the preseason, once for substances of abuse and once for performance-enhancing drugs. During the season, you will randomly be tested at your team facility, but the real fun starts in the off-season.

There are few things more uncomfortable than having someone watch you pee shirtless with your shorts below your knees in your own home. If you have stage fright, you will have to get over it quickly. Make sure you are hydrated and ready to go when the tester arrives, because sitting around your house making small talk with a guy who is there to watch you pee can get awkward pretty quickly.

What if you're not home when you are randomly selected to give a sample? It is important to know that you are responsible for letting the league know of any trips, domestic or international, you plan on taking. If for some reason you decided to stay on the uninhabited subantarctic volcanic Island of Bouvet in the South Atlantic Ocean, the NFL must know about it. Failure to be where you informed them you would be when you're called to give a urine sample will result in a failed test.

Oh, and if you've taken a banned substance and think you can hide in a remote part of the world as long as you've informed the NFL, you're wrong. Whether by land, sea, or air, they'll make sure they find a tester who can get to you.

ADVICE: However you relieve yourself when you use the throne is your business, but what if you can't "hose the porcelain" without "bombing the bowl" while a stranger watches you during a mandatory drug test? Well . . . that's the drug collector's business now too. Advice for this situation? Just smile and try to let it go; this awkward circumstance happens more often than you think. Have fun!

KNOW YOUR OPTIONS:
BYE WEEK

Bye week is a chance to catch your breath, get healthy, and spend time reviewing your team's performance up to this point. Use this time wisely. There is no right answer for how to spend it, but don't be an idiot.

Weigh your options carefully. Injured? You better stay in town getting treatment at the facility. Use the bye week to clear your mind and heal your body. There is plenty of time in the offseason to let loose . . . the season is for doing work.

SOME OF YOUR TEAMMATES MIGHT DO THE FOLLOWING:

- Fly home to visit/brag with family and friends
- Fly back to their alma mater to catch a game (hoping to get on the sidelines)
- Stay in town and watch movies
- Stay in town and fly in a "friend" for a few nights
- Vegas trip

SOME OF YOUR UNINTELLIGENT TEAM-MATES MIGHT DO THE FOLLOWING:

- Spend money on a trip they can't afford
- Take a trip to the Bahamas and come back overweight and out of shape
- Get a DUI (see section on quickest ways to get cut)
- Beat somebody up who disrespected them
- Vegas trip

QUICKEST WAYS TO
GET CUT

Not playing well enough during training camp or preseason games? A team with a stacked depth chart and an abundance of good players at your position? Schemes that don't fit well with your skill set? These are normal reasons guys get cut. Want to get cut quicker? Try some of these moves:

HURT THE QB

It doesn't matter if you fall into his legs during practice, get too close and have your helmet break his hand on a follow-through, or fight him in the locker room. They wear red jerseys for a reason. Hurt that player and not only are you out of a job, but fans might come for your head.

SKIPPING CURFEW

Nothing shows less regard for your job than trying to sneak out of the hotel the night before the game for a little fun. It signals to the coaches and management that you care more about partying or girls than football, and, if you are caught, it will likely signal the end of your time with the team.

GET A DUI

Why players in professional sports continue to get DUIs is baffling. Many clubs offer free car services and most players can afford it! Yet, every year, someone decides to embarrass their team, family, and themselves by drinking and driving. Oh, and let's not forget all the lives you put in danger with this selfish decision.

MEDIA CALLOUT

You don't have to like what the decision makers of your team are doing, but you need to respect them, especially publicly. Well, you don't, but question the head coach, GM, or owner to the media and watch how quickly your locker gets packed up in boxes.

THROW ME THE @#%$&! BALL!

ACT LIKE A PRIMA DONNA

So you just saw the All-Pro receiver yelling at the offensive coordinator to "Throw him the damn ball!" He also cursed out the QB, his position coach, the equipment staff, trainers, and anyone else who walked near him. He might get away with it, but you won't. Not a good idea to follow suit.

INAPPROPRIATE RELATIONSHIPS

This should be common sense, but spouses, significant others, or offspring of your coworkers are off limits. Unsuitable relationships with these people will cause a great deal of turmoil in the locker room and likely signal a fast exit for the player involved.

INSIDE THE LOCKER ROOM

TAKING A
SHOWER PILL

The "shower pill" is code for players who decide not to shower after a light practice or walk-through. Shouting, "Hey! (Player name)'s got shower pills!" is meant to reveal those teammates of yours with poor hygiene. So just take a shower. At the very least, rinse off. And never get caught "taking a shower pill" after a long, gruesome, full-padded practice, or you'll be branded a first-class dirty bird for life.

NEVER SHOWER AGAIN!

THE SHOWER PILL

DISTRIBUTED BY P.U. INDUSTRIES

NEGOTIATING
JERSEY NUMBER TRADES

You've probably heard about the free agent signing a big-money contract with a new team and then paying one of his new teammates to give up the rights to his favorite jersey number. This transaction is perfectly acceptable since the player purchasing the jersey can afford the purchase and likely has a history of wearing that number in the league.

Sadly, there have been occasions when a not-so-established player (like you) pays tens of thousands of dollars directly to another not-so-established player to procure the right to wear their favorite number. Remember that you are a rookie with no history playing professional football. There really isn't a great reason for you to spend your hard-earned cash to purchase the right to wear your favorite number. Number 84 will not help you catch more passes—catching more passes will help you catch more passes.

Now, if you are the one who has a number another player wants? Sell, sell, sell! This is a no-brainer, and, in case you need help trying to figure how to be compensated, here are a few examples of transactions that have happened over the years:

BONANZA

This wealthy player wants your number bad, but he's not giving you cash. But how would you like a luxury watch, your dreamcar, or an all-expenses-paid trip to a destination of your choice?

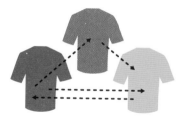

MULTI-SWAP

You may be willing to part with your number, but someone else has your true number. This may require a shuffle of jerseys with three or more players. Not impossible, but not very likely.

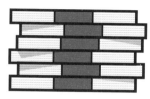

BIG MONEY

We've seen and heard of transactions ranging from $50 to $100K

DEEBO

Sometimes, a player (depending on their status) will simply just take the number from a player with no compensation whatsoever.

CHARITABLE

A player makes a large charitable donation to the charity of your choice.

GARAGE SALE

This one is strange but some transactions have consisted of random used personal belongings, ranging from portable DVD players to fishing equipment.

KITCHEN SINK

A famous player who just arrived on your team may have endorsement deals. You prefer cash, but don't be surprised if you get offered a new laptop, multiple pairs of shoes, gift cards, and six-packs of your favorite brew.

KNOW YOUR
HANDSHAKES

Much can be determined about a person by the way they shake hands. Too hard suggests they're trying to prove to you how strong and dominant they are. Too soft implies they'll probably give up easily. Over time, the handshake has evolved into many different forms. In the locker room, you have many different ways in which you may engage in a handshake.

3–5 PUMPS/FIRM GRIP

1–2 PUMPS/LIGHT GRIP

THE TRADITIONAL

Best approach when greeting the owner, head coach, general manager, and others in positions of authority. Also used for reporters and people you don't know well. Friendly, but businesslike. Firm, but not a show of strength.

THE LATE SEASON

This is a version of the "traditional" but with much softer grip pressure. Not a dead-fish handshake, but not a firm grip either. It is not a show of weakness. It can be attributed to the soreness of your hands and fingers from a season's worth of trauma.

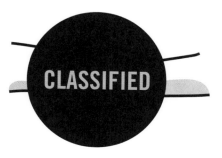

THE BRO HUG

Half handshake, half hug. This embrace is best when used on someone you don't see on a daily basis or after games. Using the bro hug too often can minimize its meaningfulness. Commonly used when greeting former teammates or coaches on the field before and after the game. (See section on After Game Opponent Mingling.) Can be used to show enthusiasm or empathy.

THE SECRET HANDSHAKE

Only used with your closest friends.

BONES

Good greeting to use with informal acquaintances. Minimizes hand pain, especially if it is late in the season. Also limits germ transfer, because ball players are dirty creatures.

SIDE BONES

Offers maximum protection for your late-season battered knuckles. Ideal with traditional "Bones" givers who like to violently fist-bump.

PREPARE FOR THE
MUSIC WARS

The locker room is a melting pot of different personalities. Nowhere is this more apparent than in musical tastes. Every team typically has a self-appointed DJ and, depending on the culture and/or layout of the locker room, there could be multiple DJs. Sometimes, teammates will argue over what they believe the locker room wants to listen to. When that happens, usually the oldest guy in the room has final say. As a rookie, you don't get any say in what is being played. If the bass from a hip-hop beat is rattling your locker, tough. If the slow country song is putting you to sleep, bring your own headphones. Try to be open-minded. Get a little culture in your life; it may broaden your musical palette.

LOCKER-ROOM BETS:
THE FINE PRINT

As you know, athletes are very competitive in everything, even the simplest of challenges. From free-throw paper ball shoot-offs to saltine-cracker eating contests, athletes love to prove their skills in every form of competition. Savvy veterans are masters at the art of making something difficult look easy, and they love nothing more than to swindle new blood into sucker bets. Beware of the hustle. If an older player bets you lunch on who can throw a paper ball into the trash can sixty feet away, make sure you've established that you must throw it from sixty feet away. Otherwise, you'll attempt from that distance and that savvy vet will just walk right up to the trash can and throw it directly in from inches away. If you decide to make a wager with a veteran, make sure you understand all the details of the fine print.

WHAT TO KNOW ABOUT
NICKNAMES

Listen, everybody gets nicknames and sometimes more than one. Usually it's an act of endearment. Some of them are good, some are bad, but you're best off not putting up a fight to any nicknames because the more you show you dislike them, the more likely they are to stick. A bad nickname likely won't last, but the right nickname can stick with you your entire career. A nickname isn't always a bad thing, either. It can help advance your career simply by giving you an identity over the many unmemorable names of players competing against you.

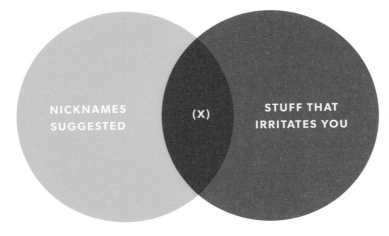

(X) NICKNAME THAT STICKS

Obese defensive lineman who loved to walk around shirtless. Everyone asked him to cover up his "bad body" but he refused, thus earning him this unflattering nickname for life.

Cro-Magnon-like facial features with long hair and beard. Simple yet unforgettable.

Extremely well-built pro-football specimen, but once you asked him to do any athletic movement, he moved stiffer than a G.I. Joe.

Limited talent, unlike the famous superhero. Not exactly Steve Rogers, but this guy gave the coach loud, military-esque responses and went hard every single drill and play.

If you miss a practice, it's a hefty fine. If you miss a lot of practices and don't seem to care? You've now been named after the famous high school wise-guy movie character determined to have a day off from school.

Large protruding forehead made this player an easy target to compare to the unmistakably unique beluga whale.

BE PREPARED:
THE STADIUM TOUR

Every fan wants to know what it's like inside the doors of an NFL team facility. Luckily for them, many teams offer such an opportunity. From time to time you will see behind-the-scenes tours being given to kids, sponsors, charity groups, etc. When these tours take place during your workday, those in attendance tend not to see you as a person, but, rather, more like a zoo animal. Expect to hear conversations about you within earshot, requests made that are beyond common courtesy, and pictures to be taken of you in your natural habitat.

A SAMPLING OF
PRANKS, JOKES,
& SHENANIGANS

One of the most enjoyable parts of being an NFL player is getting to take part in all the foolishness that happens on the practice field, in the meeting rooms, and in the locker room. A mundane day can quickly become exciting from a well-timed prank on an unsuspecting victim. Older players will sometimes scheme for days, even weeks, to catch you off-guard. Here are some of our favorites:

HOTHEAD
A generous rub of pain-relieving balm in the target's helmet. They won't notice until it's too late and they feel the heat.

CUT LACES
You may not notice the sneaky snip of the laces on your cleats with the trainer's scissors until you're ready to hit the field.

Hey, coach, I love the smell of your musk after practice.

WHAT?!!

CODEBREAKER
Make sure your phone has a great password and is on lockdown. Teammates having access to your phone can get you into big trouble.

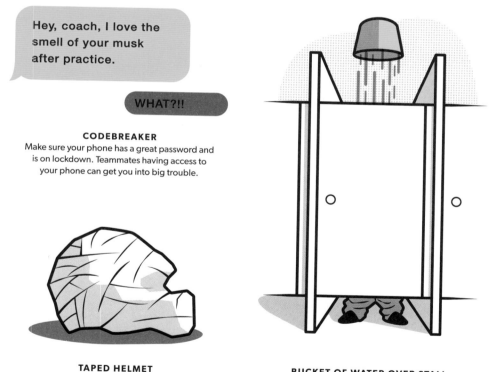

TAPED HELMET
Believe it or not, there's a football helmet in there under mountains of trainer's tape. If you're not careful, it might be yours and right as you're supposed to be hitting the practice field.

BUCKET OF WATER OVER STALL
If you're enjoying a little "me time" in the bathroom stall, be on the lookout for a full bucket of cold water coming your way.

LOOSE WATER BOTTLE CAP

Practice is intense and the sun is blazing. You're tired, you're thirsty, you need to cool off. A friendly veteran offers you a cold drink. Unbeknownst to you, the lid was unscrewed and now you are on the receiving end of the entire contents of the bottle.

AC CONFETTI

Better hope the temperature in your car is exactly how you like it. Otherwise, if you turn on the AC, you might get an early preview of what winning the Super Bowl feels like.

BUBBLE WRAP

Since you were a kid, Bubble Wrap has been fun to pop. It's not so fun, however, to remove it from your vehicle after a prankster veteran just wrapped your entire car in it.

SALTY GARNISH

You set your lunch down at a table amongst friends, but you forgot to grab utensils. Don't be shocked when your "friends" decide to improve your rice with a generous serving of table salt while you're away.

TOWEL WHIPPING

An oldie but a goodie. Pro tip: A slightly wet towel (one that has been used to dry off) is more deadly.

DAVY JONES'S LOCKER

Where did all the personal items from your locker go? You should probably check to see if they are anchored down by weights at the bottom of the cold tub.

JACKPOT JACKASS

No, you did not just win $300 million. You were given a fake lottery ticket. Hope you didn't just quit and curse out that coach who's been riding you all season.

HIDDEN TRAVEL CLOTHES

When you're on the road, make sure you keep your travel clothes safe and secure. The coaches don't want to hear your excuses when you're late for the team bus.

MYSTERY SHOE STEW

Always check your shoes before blindly plopping your hooves in. You never know what might find its way inside.

LIVE ANIMALS

You need to call local animal control services. Your locker just became a small petting zoo.

ROOM SERVICE SURPRISE

When traveling on the road, don't be surprised to have an expensive meal show up to your room . . . on you, of course.

TAILOR-MADE

You may think your clothes are fine just the way they are, but your new secret seamstress decided that nice shirt of yours needed a few new holes for aeration.

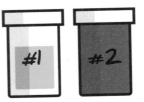

RANDOM DRUG TEST

Your athletic trainers have no idea why you just brought them a container of your urine and stool. Did you really think an official drug tester would just leave two empty containers and a note at the door of your training camp dorm room?

RESERVED
**TABLE
FOR ONE**

TABLE FOR ONE

You've spotted a group of guys you'd like to fellowship with during lunch. There's an open chair at the table and right as you're sitting down . . . the entire group stands up in unison and leaves. No one is safe from the embarrassing table-ditch move, not even coaches.

SNOWMOBILE

There's a strong chance that mother nature did not bury your car with that huge mound of snow.

CLASSIC HALF NECKTIE

Don't fall asleep on that long plane ride. When you wake, you may find yourself looking for the bottom half of your freshly cut tie.

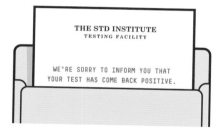

COUNTERFEIT LETTERHEAD

They sure look legit, with fancy letterheads and envelopes. Make sure it's the real deal before you follow up on that $35,000 fine from the league office, the letter from your alma mater explaining how your degree's been revoked, or that note from the team doctor stating your blood test shows you've tested positive for an STD.

SOAP GRENADE

Watch out! As you're drying off from a nice warm shower, an excessive amount of liquid soap is being hurled at your back. You now have to rinse and repeat. You didn't think the shower was safe from tomfoolery, did you?

PERMANENT MARKER

Coach is out of the room and the oldest player just handed you a marker and told you to go to the board and draw a funny picture of coach. There's no harm in a funny little drawing, unless you've been duped into doing it with a permanent marker.

EVICTION NOTICE

You should never retaliate against a veteran player, especially one who has the resources to hire a moving company to pack your entire house and put it in public storage.

CAR ON BLOCKS

This teammate has taken it too far, but regardless, you still need to find a ride home . . . and your tires!

SECTION 15

PUBLIC LIFE

THE IMPORTANCE OF
SECURITY

Professional athletes are often ideal targets for thieves. Since your schedule is public, burglars know exactly when you won't be home. Get a decent security system. Also, identity theft is a real threat, especially for someone whose personal details are scattered about the internet for all to find. Get out your wallet and buy a service that monitors for fraudulent activities.

ADVICE:
Never use the same signature for personal documents that you do for autographing memorabilia for fans.

QUICK TIPS ON
DATING

You're probably starting to think you're a big deal now that you're in the big leagues. Well, you're not alone, because there's someone out there who just might agree. Use caution when dating someone who seems to like your lifestyle and your status as an NFL player more than they like you. How can you tell? Here are a few types you should probably avoid dating and some early signs to identify them:

COACH'S OFFSPRING

Unless you plan on marrying into the family, probably not a good idea. Your failure or success with the team might not be affected by the relationship, but public perception will. (Also, see section on quickest ways to get cut.) Red flag: the same last name as coach!

THE GOLD DIGGER

The Gold Digger is very cunning and knows how to blind you to their swindling act. Stay guarded and keep track of your wallet. Red flags: a prowess for designer clothes and jewelry. Will ask for financial help in a very seductive way.

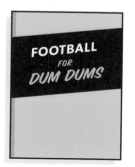

❤ 78 Likes

jerzeechsr hangin' at the big team party! #lookatme

view all 23 comments

sportsgrrl so jealous!

CLUELESS SPORTS FAN

Maybe you find someone who doesn't care for sports and really likes you for you and not what you do. Be watchful, though, of someone who is persistently reminding you that they neither follow nor like sports. You might be getting played by a Jersey Chaser incognito. Red flags: overboard with disinterest.

THE JERSEY CHASER

A bit of attention-seekers, Jersey Chasers care more about the celebrity lifestyle than the money. They make their appearances at games and team functions extremely visible on social media.

Red flags: readily available. Follows an excessive number of professional athletes on social media.

REPRESENTING
YOUR TEAM

TEAM APPEARANCES

Your new franchise will undoubtedly ask you to take part in a number of different events such as pep rallies, building playgrounds, visiting hospitals, engaging with the military, or schmoozing with corporate partners. Your team has a vested interest in getting involved in the community, so represent yourself and the organization well. If you're dreading doing another corporate event, try to view it as an opportunity to expand your network and meet some well-connected members of your local community. Should this football gig not work out, you might need these contacts to help you find a new job.

TEAM PHILANTHROPY

In addition to your mandatory appearances on behalf of the team, your teammates will have charitable causes and youth football camps of their own, and they'll want you to be involved. These events are important; however, they will cut into your free time. You should absolutely help, but be selective. While some players are really making a difference, others are doing it strictly for the image and PR. Try to commit to those in your locker room who are making a real impact. Also, if you ask teammates to help you raise money or awareness for your cause, then you better show up for theirs.

TEAM APPAREL

The equipment staff will issue you an abundance of gear peppered with logos of your squad. This gear is meant to be worn freely during practices, games, workouts, meetings, and sometimes team functions. It is even tolerable to wear old gear around the house. Team apparel is *not* meant to be worn to the grocery store, restaurants, bars, clubs, or any other public place to draw attention to yourself and brag to strangers that you play in the NFL. Not only is it tacky, but it comes off as desperate and vain.

LYING ABOUT
YOUR JOB

The locals love their team, and these fans get really excited seeing their favorite players out and about town. Sometimes, when a fan engages you, they aren't always certain you are who they think you are. They either partially recognize you or assume you play football because of your size and build.

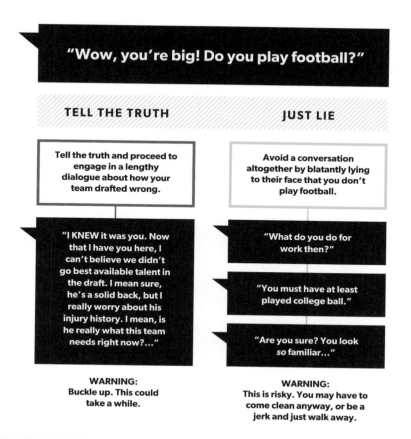

"Wow, you're big! Do you play football?"

TELL THE TRUTH

Tell the truth and proceed to engage in a lengthy dialogue about how your team drafted wrong.

"I KNEW it was you. Now that I have you here, I can't believe we didn't go best available talent in the draft. I mean sure, he's a solid back, but I really worry about his injury history. I mean, is he really what this team needs right now?…"

WARNING:
Buckle up. This could take a while.

JUST LIE

Avoid a conversation altogether by blatantly lying to their face that you don't play football.

"What do you do for work then?"

"You must have at least played college ball."

"Are you sure? You look *so* familiar…"

WARNING:
This is risky. You may have to come clean anyway, or be a jerk and just walk away.

STEREOTYPES

As you trek through the strange and amazing world that is professional football, you will undoubtedly encounter characters who range from interesting to bizarre. These are some of the various stereotypes you will encounter in most, if not all, NFL locker rooms.

THE GHOST LIFTER

This individual either doesn't feel the need to get stronger or is just flat-out lazy. The Ghost Lifter is a master at looking busy in the weight room. They create the illusion they are doing the same mandatory lifts as the rest of the team. But while some players are straining on their last set of reps in the squat rack, the Ghost Lifter is busy completing three sets of walking around and chitchat. Ghost Lifters are easy to spot; look for someone with little to no sweat wearing a towel around their neck. They are also somehow one or two lifts ahead and finish way before you do. The Ghost Lifter typically has plenty of natural strength, so they can manage cutting corners in the interim. Everyone has ghost-lifted at least once in their careers, but years of ghost lifting? That'll catch up to you on the back end.

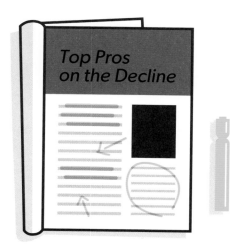

PRESS CLIPPINGS COACH

Your coach just informed you that the local paper graded your performance last week and you received a D+. Don't read that crap! Coach says that national blog he despises just wrote a piece on how pathetic you were on special teams this year. They don't know what they're talking about, so tune it out! Coach just asked if you happened to catch that segment channel 4 did last night on how you're a bust. You didn't see it? Good.

This coach doesn't want you to read or hear anything that might negatively affect your confidence, except . . . this coach is inadvertently reading or telling you everything that might negatively affect your confidence.

BFF COACH

This is not the same as a player's coach. This coach is worried about the influence you might have over their job security. Limited constructive criticism with concerns that, if they're too hard on you, then you may get upset and try to get 'im fired. Hopefully you don't get paired with this coach. It might make reviewing a bad game tape easier to sit through, but in the long run, this coach won't make you better and will probably get fired anyway.

BIG SPENDERS

Every locker room in the league is comprised of individuals who are eager to flaunt their status with lavish purchases. From rare basketball shoes and fancy timepieces to exotic sports cars and upscale hotels, these individuals only own the most exclusive, high-end, quality stuff. Simple fact: Professional athletes make good money, but just because you've spent the last few years rationing your college per diem doesn't mean you need to own every bag Louis Vuitton makes.

SING-ALOUD PLAYER

Without fail, there are players who get into the music that's piping through their headphones and can't help but sing aloud so everyone can hear. They sing obnoxiously and are generally among the most attention-seeking members of the team. There is a reason you have on headphones. It's so everyone else doesn't have to listen to your music. Fight the urge. No one wants to hear your crappy singing on the quiet ride to the stadium.

THE BACKUP QUARTERBACK

If the starting quarterback is healthy and playing well, then the backup has what some consider the best job in the world. He usually plays a lot of golf, gets paid well, doesn't have the stress of a starter, has the best seat in the house on game days, and, best of all . . . wears a red jersey in practice, signifying that no one can hit him! Usually the fans of the team also view the backup as better than he truly is, oftentimes calling for the coach to put him in over the struggling starter. Generally, this player is a veteran. If so, look to him for some extra advice or guidance, as well as hilarious stories and gossip concerning famous coaches and players around the league.

THE LONG SNAPPER

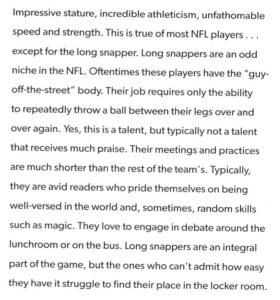

Impressive stature, incredible athleticism, unfathomable speed and strength. This is true of most NFL players . . . except for the long snapper. Long snappers are an odd niche in the NFL. Oftentimes these players have the "guy-off-the-street" body. Their job requires only the ability to repeatedly throw a ball between their legs over and over again. Yes, this is a talent, but typically not a talent that receives much praise. Their meetings and practices are much shorter than the rest of the team's. Typically, they are avid readers who pride themselves on being well-versed in the world and, sometimes, random skills such as magic. They love to engage in debate around the lunchroom or on the bus. Long snappers are an integral part of the game, but the ones who can't admit how easy they have it struggle to find their place in the locker room.

THE PLAYER REP

The NFLPA is a union that represents the interests of the players. Every team votes for one player on their roster to be its representative. Team owners typically despise the reps. Their duties are to organize union meetings, keep players up to speed on all union/ league matters, and answer any questions you may have regarding your benefits. Don't hold your breath, though; they usually don't have the answers you need and will always ask to "get back to you." Eventually you'll get a response on the resources you've inquired about, probably once your rep returns from the annual union meeting in Hawaii that is paid for by your union dues.

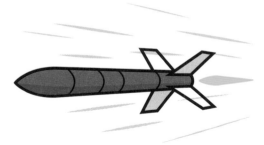

SPECIAL-TEAMS ACE

This player is found on every team in professional football. Wasn't a star player in college but loves playing football. Good athlete and likely a little bit crazy. Special-Teams Aces play smart with great effort and reckless abandon for their bodies. They look forward to sprinting fifty yards for a full-speed, head-on collision. Not much of a role on offense or defense, but does a good job on the scout team during the week. May also have an obsession with yoga and healthy dieting.

STEREOTYPES

TURN-THE-PAGE PLAYER

It's perfectly normal to be proud of your school. But walking around every day with a jumpsuit, ball cap, backpack, and custom shoes in your alma mater's colors and logos is too much. Don't be this player; it's a sad obsession. Besides, no one cares that you upset forty-third-ranked Middle Nevada State your junior year.

FREQUENT SPEECH PLAYER

Motivating a group of grown men is a challenge. Players long in the tooth of their pro careers have heard countless hours of "rah-rah" type messages. Frequent Speech Players love to talk about how they did it in college or another team they were on. They want you to know how much they train and how no one in the world wants it more than they do. They especially like to remind everyone about all the hardships they've been through in football and in life.

Some players feel the need to constantly rally the troops and share their self-proclaimed gift of verbal expression. Typically, the guy who gives all the speeches is not the same guy players look to for leadership . . . unless that person is William Wallace.

THE SABOTAGE VET

Many players will happily mentor you if you ask. Some players might not oblige because they are selfish, have little patience, are too busy with their own struggles, or feel threatened of their job security since you play their same position. Although rare, there are also some players who will purposely give you poor advice and misinformation. They don't want you to succeed because your success is their demise. Be wary of who you seek out for guidance. The Sabotage Vet is typically arrogant with a false sense of confidence. An early sign is someone who tries to verbally humiliate you and often gives you the wrong answer for a play assignment.

THE SWISS ARMY LINEMAN

Each team is allowed only forty-five players on game days, which means most teams dress only seven offensive linemen. At least one of the backup offensive linemen will have to be a Swiss Army knife, jack-of-all-trades-type player. Roles can and will include backing up multiple spots on the offensive line, playing tight end in short yardage and goal-line situations, blocking on kickoff returns and field goal attempts, and/or being the emergency long snapper. If this Swiss Army Lineman is a trusted veteran, it is also likely that this person stands next to the line coach while the offense is on the field, acting as an extra set of eyes and sometimes even amateur psychiatrist. These players are generally intelligent and willing to help the team in any capacity they can. Coaches love to have this type of player around and the Swiss Army Lineman can be found on almost every roster.

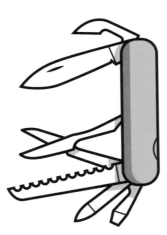

AUTOGRAPH HOUND

Asking for an autograph from a teammate can sometimes be awkward, especially when asking the famous players who get requests quite often. Rounding up signed memorabilia is never awkward for the autograph hound. This player, typically inactive, forgets to go holiday shopping and needs some last-minute footballs signed by his superstar teammates. It's OK to get an occasional ball signed for a charity event or yourself, but don't be the guy who spends his time in the locker room chasing around the stars for their John Hancock.

COACH'S PET

Coach's Pets go out of their way to try to impress the coach off the field. In the facility, this player is constantly found conversing with the coach about personal matters in the hope of creating a relationship that will make it hard for the coach to consider cutting that player. In meetings, this player is always the first to yell out answers to open questions meant for the entire room, and many times will answer when the question was for someone else. During film review of practice, this player makes sure to call attention to their best plays by saying things like "Hey, coach, did I do this right?" when that player damn well knows that they did it right.

Don't be this guy. You'll lose the respect of your coach and your teammates. If you want to impress everyone, do it with the way you perform on the gridiron.

THE WORKOUT WARRIOR

No matter how much time they spend in the weight room doing extra curls or conveniently doing yoga when the head coach walks by, the Workout Warrior just does not possess enough talent to play on Sundays. That's why the Workout Warrior spends so much time in the gym. If they can't get in the game because of their lack of football savvy, then at least they'll look good in a uniform. Ironically, the Workout Warrior may get multiple tryouts just for looking the part.

JOURNEYMAN PLAYER

A Journeyman Player has bounced from team to team trying to find a permanent home. This nomad might even be a really good player but, for whatever reason, has yet to be given the opportunity to prove it. The Journeyman has no loyalty to the team because of his history of rejection, but he does have a great pulse on the facilities, culture, and personalities of many franchises around the league.

THE DOUBLE-CROSS COACH

The Double-Cross Coach is a rarity in the league, but they do exist. This coach will teach you to do one thing, but if it turns out to be wrong they will deny any culpability and might even scold you in front of the head coach to save face.

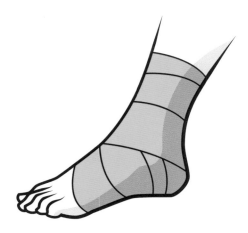

MILKMAN INJURY PLAYER

This player doesn't have a desire and/or ability to make the team, so they either fake an injury or pretend an existing one is worse than it really is. Typically, an agent educates the player, convincing them that the team can't cut them while they are still injured. This is purely a money-grab move that provides the player (and agent) a few more weeks of income until the team agrees to a settlement. It's a lot easier to pretend you want to play in the NFL than to actually play in the NFL.

FORMER PLAYERS

MOST PLAYERS BELIEVE THAT FOOTBALL IS NOT WHO THEY ARE — IT'S WHAT THEY DO. THEY SOON FIND OUT WHAT THAT REALLY MEANS WHEN IT'S TIME TO HANG UP THEIR CLEATS. IN TIME, YOU'LL MEET SOME OF THESE FORMER PLAYERS IN THEIR NEW REALITIES . . . OR EVENTUALLY BE ONE YOURSELF.

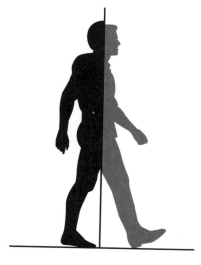

IN LIMBO

These players have trouble finding an identity in their new reality. They're not quite sure if they should truly retire from the game, go back to school, look for a new occupation, or write a book about football. Even though they're no longer part of the team they still have friends who play, but those relationships are now very different.

COMMENTATOR

The former player now turned commentator becomes more of a legend in their mind with each passing season. These players often complained about the unfair criticism toward their play but now have no problem judging current players or pretending to know a current player's reads and responsibilities. Next time you turn on the tube, listen for the former player commentator's go-to line: "You know, back when I played . . . "

ASSISTANT COACH

Coaching is one of the more common transitions for a former player. They either truly love the game or had nothing else to fall back on. The former player coaches love to tell you how the game has changed and how much harder it was when they played. They're also chameleons in having the uncanny ability to complain to players about coaches and complain to coaches about players.

GENERIC BUSINESSMAN

Business Ventures
Worlwide Incorporated
"Our business is business"

Generic businessmen dabble in multiple businesses or none at all. If they do have a small stake in some type of venture, they typically have no idea what that business does. They are all about networking and building relationships but have no business prospects or commerce to speak of. Clean-cut, sharply attired, they give the illusion of success but under the surface are still looking for an identity.

SECTION 17
POSTSEASON

PRO BOWL

Making the Pro Bowl your first year is an impressive achievement. Even if you have a great season, it's not always easy to jump a longtime, prominent pro who can sometimes get voted in on name and reputation alone. Trading helmets and jerseys is a longtime tradition of the Pro Bowl, so make sure your equipment manager packs you extra gear to barter. Future hall of famers are likely not going to want to trade with you, so don't get your feelings hurt if they refuse to trade helmets.

Practice tempo can be similar to a walkthrough (depending on the coach) and the game might follow suit, but don't get too comfortable too soon. You never know which player will decide to take advantage of your laxness to try to win MVP so they can take home a new truck.

ADVICE:

If a well-known player you admire and have never met is asking which room you are in, it's probably not to hang out and bond. Most likely, that player is trying to make your room the official place to charge all expenses.

PLAYOFFS

Should you find yourself on a playoff team, appreciate this incredible accomplishment. Some players go their entire careers and never see the postseason. Being a part of the NFL playoffs is a thrilling experience. If you thought the speed and intensity of the regular season was fast already, wait until you see it in the fury of single-game elimination. Many players get caught up in the media hype of the playoffs. Don't read and watch what's being said about you. Instead, focus on the task at hand . . . winning and getting your squad to the 'ship.

SUPER BOWL

If you've ever been in a college bowl game, the Super Bowl experience is similar logistically. You will spend a week in a hotel practicing at someone else's facility and attend mulitple functions celebrating the big game. Playing in the Super Bowl is thrilling, but the lead-up can be incredibly distracting. Autograph hounds are rampant and the media spotlight is the brightest you've ever seen. Tickets are unbelievably expensive, not to mention limited, and everyone you know will want to go. Since your routine will obviously be changed, it's imperative to get all your planning out of the way early so you can focus on the most important thing . . . winning the game. You might never get another chance to be in the big dance.

TWO-MINUTE WARNING

NEW DWELLING

You've moved to a brand-new city and you no longer have to share a grimy, run-down shack with a horde of your college team-mates. You can afford to have a nice place all to yourself and you deserve it. You might be tempted to get a giant house in the suburbs or a fancy condo in the nicest building downtown. Don't do either, at least right away. It's okay to rent until you figure out the lay of the land. Find something that's nice but reasonable and isn't too far from the practice facility.

WEARING APPAREL OF OTHER TEAMS

Almost every person involved with professional football is a fan of the game in some capacity. We've all had a team we grew up rooting for, but now that you're being paid by one that might not be your childhood favorite, it is not okay to fly a different team's colors. Every so often some dummy thinks it's a good idea to rock a ball cap of a divisional rival just because the hat is cool.

NATIONAL ANTHEM

Being a citizen of a country that allows you to play a game for a living is a privilege. The national anthem not only reminds us of that privilege, but also honors those who sacrificed their lives to protect it. If at this point in your career you don't know proper national anthem etiquette, here are a few reminders: Step up to the white line. Take your hat off. Put your right hand over your heart, and set a good example for the young fans watching you.

MAIL/AUTOGRAPHS

Letters and autograph requests from fans young and old will be sent to you at the team facility daily. You will probably even get some letters with unwanted religious advice or business cards introducing you to a new financial planner. It might be difficult to find time to go through and respond to all of the mail you receive. Our advice—throw out anything that looks mass-produced and try to take time to sign the autograph requests or respond to the personal letters—especially when they are from kids.

SNIPERS AND CARPET MONSTERS

Most professional football players are very cognizant of their image. There are few things as amusing as when a player who struts around with swag suddenly trips or falls in the middle of practice or while walking around the facility. While they look around with concern failing to find what caused them to stumble, be alert for someone to shout: "Sniper got 'im!" or "Uh-oh, Carpet Monster!"

OUTKICKED YOUR COVERAGE

If you ever hear a coach tell you "You've outkicked your coverage," it means they think your significant other is more attractive than you are. If you've never heard that before now, not to worry, coaches use that phrase frequent and often.

SUITS

As we discussed earlier, owning a nice suit is a neccessity. Every team usually has a player or coach who recommends a "custom suit" maker. This recommendation may be due to the outstanding customer service and quality of craftsmanship that the tailor provides. If that person on your team is aggressively soliciting you to buy from no one but them . . . it means that, if you buy a suit, they get a free one. Custom suit or not, don't go crazy. Styles change. You can always spot the oldest guy in the room based on the style suit they wear. Typically, older players and coaches rock the same ill-fitting suits their entire careers.

OFF-SEASON

PARTING WORDS

Congratulations on surviving your rookie season. We hope this book has helped you avoid the common mistakes first-year players make. An NFL season is a grueling experience, but now you're in the off-season, so take some much-deserved time off to rest and recover. Enjoy your freedom away from the game, but don't become complacent. There's an entirely new class of rookies coming in next year to try to take your job.

Players like to joke that the NFL stands for Not For Long. There is a sad truth to that amusing acronym. Be grateful for the opportunity that you have worked so hard for, and make the most of it. If you care at all about the fraternity you're now a part of, pay it forward. Share this book, or, better yet, share your insights and experiences with players who come after you. Show them how to be a professional. After all, we were all rookies once.

THE ROOKIE HANDBOOK TEAM

RYAN KALIL (ROOKIE YEAR 2007)

Ryan Kalil is an All-Pro NFL center for the Carolina Panthers who was drafted in the second round of the 2007 NFL Draft. He played college football at the University of Southern California (the real USC), where he won two national championships, was named a first-team All-American, and won the 2006 Morris Trophy. In the NFL, Kalil has played nine seasons, been to five Pro Bowls, was named All-Pro in 2011, 2013 and 2015, and played in Super Bowl 50. In 2014, as part of a barbershop quartet group, Kalil sang *Happy Trails* to Jordan Gross during his retirement press conference. Ryan currently lives in Charlotte, North Carolina, with his wife, Natalie, and their three children. Ryan has long enjoyed sports, comics, and cinema (nerd alert!). When it comes to his personal wardrobe, some of his teammates refer to his style as "confused white guy."

ROOKIE HAIRCUT OF CHOICE:
THE FRIAR TUCK

JORDAN GROSS (ROOKIE YEAR 2003)

Jordan Gross is a former All-Pro NFL tackle for the Carolina Panthers who was drafted in the first round of the 2003 NFL Draft. He played college football at the University of Utah, where he was recognized as a consensus first-team All-American and finalist for the Outland Trophy. In the NFL, Gross played eleven seasons, was selected to three Pro Bowls, was named All-Pro in 2008, and played in the Super Bowl XXXVIII. In 2013, Jordan played his last season with his amigos and retired a Panther. Jordan currently lives in Charlotte, North Carolina, with his wife, Dana, and their three children. He is a self-proclaimed outdoorsman who enjoys flaunting his Saddleback leather bags and wearing medium-sized clothes (he recently lost 80 lbs.).

ROOKIE HAIRCUT OF CHOICE:
THE BLACK FRIDAY

GEOFF HANGARTNER (ROOKIE YEAR 2005)

Geoff Hangartner (nicknamed Piggy) is a former NFL Swiss Army Lineman for the Carolina Panthers and Buffalo Bills who was drafted in the fifth round of the 2005 NFL Draft. He played college football at Texas A&M, where he was named first-team All-Big 12. He scored 47 out of a possible 50 on the Wonderlic Personnel Test administered during the 2005 NFL Combine (Intelligent Jock). After four years with Panthers, Geoff signed a four-year contract with the Buffalo Bills. In 2011, Geoff returned to Carolina to finish his career with his three amigos and retire a Panther. Geoff currently lives in Austin, Texas, with his wife, Christina, and their 2 children. He's nearly a scratch golfer who enjoys boating and growing a beard.

ROOKIE HAIRCUT OF CHOICE:
SHOCK & AWE

MATT STEVENS (ROOKIE YEAR 1997)

Matt Stevens is a designer and illustrator who resides in Charlotte, North Carolina, with his wife and three kids. In early 2012, he opened the Design Office of Matt Stevens to pursue his own clients and incorporate more illustration into his daily practice. His pursuit of personal projects has led to opportunities working with many great brands. The MAX100 project, a self-published book that was sold from Düsseldorf, Germany to Dubai, UAE, led to an ongoing collaboration with Nike Global/Nike Sportswear. Select clients include Nike, Evernote, *Wired*, *The Atlantic*, *Esquire*, Facebook, Google, Pinterest, and the NFL. His football accolades include three sacks in the college intramural flag football C-League and an undefeated paper football season in the third grade. Despite growing up a Cowboys fan, twenty-five-plus years in Charlotte, North Carolina has him bleeding black and blue for the Carolina Panthers.

ROOKIE HAIRCUT OF CHOICE:
THE HERO WE DESERVE

IT'S GOOD!